The Enneagram Map to Your Deeper Self

"In this book, Sandra creates a rich experience for the reader to travel through the nine Enneagram energies with helpful mindfulness practices at each stop. The companion voices she includes allow the reader to fully immerse themselves in the energy at each of the nine types. This is a great guide for those beginning their Enneagram journey and those who want to go deeper into the essence of their being."

—Deborah Threadgill Egerton, PhD, author of *Know Justice Know Peace* and *Enneagram Made Easy*

"As an experienced Enneagram practitioner, Sandra Smith brings together considerable Enneagram wisdom in her new book, gathering helpful overviews and enriching them with personal stories and diverse companion voices to help us engage with the intimate issues about each type structure. As she tells us, however, 'insights and new learnings are stimulating and fascinating but not transformative.' Sandra adds valuable practices, inquiries, and prayers to support us in making the crucial transformational shift from type to essence. I'll turn to this helpful book of Enneagram resources again and again!"

—Belinda Gore, PhD, Enneagram coach, teacher, and author of *Finding Freedom: Understanding Our Relationships Using Object Relations and the Enneagram*

"The beauty of reading *The Enneagram Map to Your Deeper Self* is that it provides a living experience of the path author Sandra Smith uses to bring forth insights, stories (from guest writers), and practices. Each chapter supports readers in understanding the journeys we travel toward our wholeness. Sandra weaves her learned rites of passage, spiritual insights, and techniques for transformation as she brings us the power of the Enneagram Map."

> —Erlina Edwards, coexecutive director of the Narrative Enneagram organization, an IEA accredited professional, and a certified Narrative Enneagram teacher and spiritual director

"At a time when the Enneagram community seems more engaged in talking and intellectualizing about the Enneagram than actually utilizing it for growth and transformation, Sandra Smith offers this beautiful contribution to the field of Enneagram literature. While Sandra's *Enneagram Map to Your Deeper Self* contains plenty of Enneagram information organized in a very accessible form, its greater gift is the treasure chest of inquiries and practices, including type-specific ones, along with a powerful call to utilize the Enneagram for its true purpose. Thank you, Sandra, for this timely gift to the Enneagram community."

> —Lynda Roberts, past president of the International Enneagram Association and former Enneagram Institute faculty member

"Sandra Smith's *Enneagram Map to Your Deeper Self* is a portal to uncharted dimensions, where authenticity thrives. She guides us to unearth our true selves and embrace earthly wisdom. This empowering book ignites potential with tangible practices—a beacon for all seekers. Inviting this book into your world unveils a transformative journey, a gift of insight and growth. Embrace its pages, for within them, new realms of being await."

> —Catherine R. Bell, MBA, author and founder of The Awakened Company

"Sandra Smith offers us a remarkable gift that comes from her deep, attentive engagement with others and with her own life. With her beautifully grounded wisdom, insight, and compassion, she opens a welcoming door to the Enneagram, both for those who are new to it as well as those who have been working with it for a long time. I am especially grateful for how she brings practical steps to engaging the mystery and complexity of our lives as she invites us to see more clearly the presence of the sacred at the heart of it all."

—Jan Richardson, author of *Sparrow: A Book of Life and Death and Life*

"I have been so enriched by Sandra Smith's contribution to the field of the Enneagram. A masterful teacher of the narrative tradition, she brings her passion to move students from the "automatic to the authentic" in their responses to daily life. As the title suggests, people often mistake their type for who they truly are. Her unique contribution in this book is to present the voices and experiences of nineteen diverse women who tell their story of leading with their type. Smith offers practices of inquiry, engagement, sabbath-keeping, and prayer for each of the types as well as blessings. I plan to recommend this book to my spiritual directees as a rich tool for diving more deeply into their awakening."

—Marcia Wakeland, pastor and spiritual director, founder of the Listening Post of Anchorage, and author of *The Long Walk Home*

"Sandra Smith's *Enneagram Map to Your Deeper Self* guides readers in identifying themselves within the Enneagram system and in perceiving its significance to their life experiences. From this decades-long Enneagram teacher, we receive insights for affirming our complex selves while in the never-ending process of becoming. It's now my first recommendation for anyone exploring the Enneagram as an interpretive resource."

—Luther E. Smith Jr., PhD, author of *Hope is Here! Spiritual Practices for Pursuing Justice and Beloved Community*, and professor emeritus, Candler School of Theology, Emory University

The
Enneagram Map *to*
Your Deeper Self

Living beyond Your Type

SANDRA C. SMITH

Foreword by Sandra Maitri

HAMPTON ROADS

This edition first published in 2024 by Hampton Roads Publishing, an imprint of
Red Wheel/Weiser, LLC

With offices at:
65 Parker Street, Suite 7
Newburyport, MA 01950

Sign up for our newsletter and special offers by going to *www.redwheelweiser.com/newsletter*

Cover design by Sky Peck Design
Cover Enneagram illustration by Sandra Smith
Interior diagrams by Sandra Smith
Interior by Happenstance Type-O-Rama
Typeset in Adobe Caslon Pro, Adobe Jenson Pro, Barlow

ISBN: 978-1-64297-060-9

Library of Congress Cataloging-in-Publication Data

Names: Smith, Sandra C., 1957- author.
Title: The enneagram map to your deeper self : living beyond your type /
    Sandra C. Smith ; foreword by Sandra Maitri.
Description: Newburyport, MA : Hampton Roads Publishing, 2024. | Includes
    bibliographical references. | Summary: "This book is an invitation to
    see yourself as more than your personality type and to engage in
    practices that liberate you from automatic patterns. You will see how to
    deepen your use of the Enneagram in support of your spiritual life as
    well as psychological health. With clarity and consistency, this book
    shows how to understand your Enneagram type without reinforcing the
    patterns of your type"-- Provided by publisher.
Identifiers: LCCN 2024009872 | ISBN 9781642970609 (trade paperback) | ISBN
    9781612834993 (ebook)
Subjects: LCSH: Enneagram. | Self-realization.
Classification: LCC BF698.35.E54 S57 2024 | DDC 155.2/6--dc23/eng/20240515
LC record available at https://lccn.loc.gov/2024009872

Printed in the United States of America
IBI

10 9 8 7 6 5 4 3 2 1

This book is dedicated to
the Rooted Ones
in their many forms.

Contents

HEAD TYPES

PART THREE

Foreword

It's no accident that the focus of much of the teaching and writing about the ancient system of the Enneagram focuses exclusively on the ins and outs of the nine types of ego structures. When the system first became widely popularized in the 1980s, it was as a typology, rather than as a key for opening us up to what lies beyond these nine egoic or personality types. This focus on the ego is a characteristic of the ego itself: it's all about maintaining the status quo of our ongoing sense of self. So we learn about our personality type, and the insights this understanding offers serve (for most people) to reinforce their sense of who they are, as an ego.

The Enneagram, however, is part of a vast teaching on the transformation of human consciousness—a teaching that focuses on the radical shift of who we know ourselves to be from the limitations and constrictions of the ego or personality, to the spiritual depths that lie beyond. I wrote my first book, *The Spiritual Dimension of the Enneagram: Nine Faces of the Soul*, to reconnect understanding of the Enneagram with this, its original and central function.

I was part of Claudio Naranjo's first Seekers After Truth (SAT) group, in which the teaching of the Enneagram as it is known today is rooted. The Enneagram was inseparable from the group's central purpose: to awaken each of us from the sleep of our egoic sense of reality. *The Enneagram Map to Your Deeper Self: Living Beyond Your Type* is likewise rooted in the deep human urge for freedom. Liberation, as all spiritual teachings tell us, is fundamentally about moving beyond our inner constraints. Outer freedom only provides the context for fulfilling this longing of the human heart. This book provides sound guidance in addressing this yearning to open ourselves to more of what we are.

Sandra Smith's orientation is steeped in this endeavor, as is that of many of the voices that speak through this book. Her teaching about the Enneagram comes to life through the contributing narratives of the companion voices of each Ennea-type. The guest contributors come from diverse backgrounds and ethnicities. They are diverse in gender orientation, functions in the world, religious and spiritual backgrounds—and none of them are the stereotypes normally presented of each type. This shows us how universal the Enneagram is to human experience. It also allows us to hear the voices and experiences of those we might not ordinarily hear from.

These contributors describe through their lived experiences how their Ennea-types have functioned in their lives, as well as what has helped them grow and move beyond the confines of their type. Their personal stories are all articulate demonstrations of a depth of self-knowledge and of inner development. They bring each type to life in a way that generalized descriptions cannot. I heartily agree with Sandra when she says, "Learning from someone living in the territory of the type is by far more insightful than studying the map or reading a generic description in a book."

The diversity of Sandra's own lived experience and background, as well as her intelligence and well of inner faith, shine throughout this book. She is obviously steeped in knowledge about the Enneagram as a result of studying with a range of its most prominent teachers, with differing orientations. And she has clearly digested this multifaceted understanding in her own soul through her years of working with the system. Her chapter on the triads contained within the Enneagram, for instance, covers views drawn from the

Armenian mystic G.I. Gurdjieff, the psychoanalyst Karen Horney, and the Enneagram teacher Dr. David Daniels, as well as a view of the Enneagram from the perspective of Harmonics informed by the teachings of Russ Hudson.

Her deep relationship with nature, her background in theology, her mediation and teaching experience, her work with others, and her engagement in the spiritual path of the Diamond Approach give this book practical groundedness, imbue it with heartfulness and compassion, and support us in opening to the Sacred.

—SANDRA MAITRI
Carmel Valley, California
January 2024

Introduction

In the summer of 1991, a T-shirt changed my life. I was between my first and second years in theology school and was on the summer staff at Ring Lake Ranch, a spiritual retreat center in the Wyoming wilderness. One morning, a guest entered the dining hall wearing a tee shirt stating, "Hi, I'm a One." Curiosity nudged me to inquire about Oneness, as it seemed like a good thing to be. Thus began my engagement with the Enneagram System, completely mistyping myself while reading the guest's Enneagram book!

Thirty-plus years later, I can truly say this system has been life-changing for me. Equipped with a map of my inner landscape of automatic patterns, fears, false inner narratives, and inherent strengths, I have a clearer view of the numerous ways I live in automatic response and miss the wonder of each moment. Given this map of information, I can choose to shift from behaviors that trip me up toward more life-giving ways of being in the world.

Over the years, my understanding of the nine types has deepened. Since becoming a Certified Narrative Enneagram Teacher I have taught and consulted on the Enneagram System for decades, and for several years I have co-hosted the *Heart of the Enneagram* podcast. Years of working with corporate leaders, nonprofit directors and staff, faith communities, therapists, coaches, and spiritual directors have taught me that *the Enneagram is complex!* It has been a privilege to witness the growth of those who take ownership of themselves and engage in transformative work with both desire and devotion. Moving from life lived on automatic to authentic living is a lifetime process, and we are worth it.

This book is the product of insights gleaned through years of listening to and observing myself and others in countless presentations and webinars and thousands of individual consults. Without realizing it, I've been carried to this moment, to this writing endeavor.

"Who am I?" is a foundational question for our spiritual lives. Without self-awareness, navigating our lives and relationships is difficult at best, because we are lost to ourselves, unavailable. A vacancy sign hangs on our metaphoric door. We feel a strong magnetic pull to focus outward. We remain in busy mode, over-planning, over-engaging, defined by others and driven by the their agendas and expectations. We live on automatic; our ability to *feel* the emotions that arise, the sensations and wisdom of our bodies, and think with clarity remains underdeveloped.

A map to assist in understanding ourselves would be so helpful, right? Our first exposure to the Enneagram System or Map can be astounding. It's an incredible experience to read about ourselves in a chapter of a book: "Wow, I'm not alone. Others are like me!" we think. And there is a modicum of truth in this—but while the Enneagram offers such a powerful laser focus into our inner workings that we may be seduced into thinking our type is who we are, that's not true. As Sandra Maitri often states, we are not our Enneagram type!

If I'm not my type, you may be wondering, then who am I, and how is the Enneagram useful to me? This question is where this book begins. We want to *understand our type and how it operates in our lives, but not reinforce the patterns of our type.* The Enneagram indicates our preferences that drive us until we become aware of these preferences and patterns. Awareness brings us the gift of choice. Do we remain in the comfort zone of the familiar, or move beyond it? In moving beyond these patterns, we begin to see that we are more than we thought we were. We begin to surprise our-selves. Each time we step out of our comfort zone, the call to live authentically in our full dimensionality is heard more clearly. And, at times, our radiance shines forth, reminding us to be open to life's delightful surprises.

I can't imagine my spiritual life without knowing the Enneagram. Knowledge of this system and how my specific type operates has given me a better understanding of how I block my heart from loving. Using the Enneagram as a guide, I see the ways I restrain and close off my heart to resist being vulnerable.

I'll offer an example of working to shift one of my behaviors as it relates to vulnerability, my core avoidance as one who leads with type Eight. The vice of this type is lust, an energy that lures me into deciding or acting *now!* Lust is a mover and a shaker. It prefers a forward movement, and I often find myself literally leaning forward. But the drive to get things done "now" can be quite wearing on myself as well as others around me. My practice of sitting back in my seat, feeling the back of the chair supporting me and feeling my feet on the ground, allows me to wait a bit longer. Waiting feels vulnerable to Eights, and anxiety arises. Yet, I honor myself by practicing "later." Staying with my breath and the felt sense of this energy helps me in this process of waiting. The desire to "get 'er done now," to feel that juice of task completion, remains with me, but with growing con-sciousness I need not act on this compulsion.

The great mystic and teacher Dr. Howard Thurman calls this urge to be constantly active and moving forward a "deadly magic." Indeed, it has been for me. Acting now negates presence. Without presence, I'm not available to myself. Slowly, I'm learning the power of patience. My practice of waiting until later allows me to get presence, and to have more energy later in the day for engaging in relationships, play, and relaxing without exhaustion. I'm not so threadbare at day's end. In the waiting, I return to myself and my heart has the space to open a bit.

Why This Book, and Why Now?

The explosion of popularity of the Enneagram has led many people to have a superficial understanding of this powerful map. But the constant reduction of humanity to memes for each Enneagram type in social media and books serves to limit a deeper understanding, dampen curiosity, and push people to make judgments. Boxing individuals in with caricatures is the opposite of what effective use of the Enneagram Map offers. As we engage with the Enneagram, if we aren't becoming more curious and compassionate, we are misunderstanding the system. The more we learn about and experience each of the Enneagram types, the more expansive our understanding becomes, and we realize that the only appropriate response to ourselves and each other is compassion. Internally, we all must navigate inner stories that lead us astray, habits that deaden our aliveness, and energy that pulls us away from presence. However, we humans are full of mystery and resilience. We can change. Remaining open to the wonder of ourselves and others is both gift and grace.

The Enneagram is more than a typing system. Discerning our type is not the end goal; it's our entry point into navigating the Enneagram Map of our ego structure. To stop the exploration after "getting our number" is to find the trailhead but not take the hike! Instead, having identified our type, we must begin exploring our inner landscape: the challenging and beautiful parts of ourselves. This book supports readers who want to engage in these inner adventures and who are open to having stereotypes challenged through reading its various contributors' experiences of their own types. The Latin root of the word respect, *respectus*, means to *look back at* or *to look again*. I invite readers to look again with fresh eyes in their exploration of the nine Enneagram types. Learning about ourselves is an endless process, and this is our magnificent work. The more we learn, the more expansive these nine types become. May compassion offer guidance as we deepen our understanding of the complex inner workings of humanity.

This book is:

An invitation to see ourselves as more than we believe we are

An invitation to learn and engage in practices that liberate us from automatic patterns

A support for dissolving stereotypes and congealed thinking about the Enneagram types

A resource for professionals working with individuals seeking personal and spiritual growth

A practical guide for softening the grip of our Enneagram type

This book is not:

An explanation of the history and origins of the Enneagram Personality System

A definitive explanation of the nine types

An academic discussion of psychology

Companion Voices

As this book was forming, the idea of including companion voices came into my consciousness like a bright light. My training in the Narrative Enneagram demonstrated the power of learning from those who live "in the skin of" an Enneagram type. In my own Enneagram teaching, learning from the lived experiences of those who represent each of the types has served to deepen my compassion. We all gain great value from hearing the "stories," the realness of a person's understanding of themselves. As Enneagram teachers like to say, "the Enneagram is a map, and each of us lives in the territory of type." Learning from someone living in the territory of the type is by far more insightful than studying the map or reading a generic description in a book. These companion voices, their humanity and perspectives, add to the teaching of the types in Part Two of this book. Their stories are glimpses into the lives of people seeking to live authentically.

My participation in Diversity, Equity, Inclusion (DEI) training, and my own identity as a lesbian, brought an intentionality to inviting those whose voices may not be heard in our culture as often as other voices to contribute. The companion writers in this book include people who are nonbinary, lesbian, bisexual, cisgender, women of color, and white women, all of whom share their life experiences leading with particular Enneagram types. These writers have various faith perspectives. Each has a unique approach to expressing their lived experience of their type. Whether in narrative or essay form, each voice offers a glimpse into type patterns as well as the daily supports and awareness that lead to growth. The late Black feminist writer Audre Lorde said decades ago in a radio interview, "When we define ourselves, when I define myself, the place in which I am like you and the place in which I am not like you, I'm not excluding you from the joining—I'm broadening the joining."[1] Over the years, Lorde's book *Sister Outsider* has been a strong reminder to me to be courageous in my claiming of myself.

Gratefulness abounds to these companion contributors for articulating and sharing their own insights and stories of growth relating to their types through their writing. Each one expanded my aware-ness and deepened my compassion. My hope is that, whoever you are, this book will provide fresh insights into our common human experience as we celebrate our internal diversity.

As I wrote this book, I was accompanied by several inner com-panion voices: those of my mentors who taught me, supported me, and shaped my initial Enneagram learning. Helen Palmer and Dr. David Daniels, co-founders of the Narrative Enneagram Tradition, quickly earned my trust as teachers who were curious, nonjudging, and wise. Witnessing these two mentors lead panels of the nine types, I learned the role of compassion in teaching and in learning. The timing of their questions, the pauses, and their model-ing of when to challenge and when to affirm students provided rich lessons. Dr. Daniels continued with me as a conversation partner over the years, offering me guidance until his unexpected death in 2017. On the faculty at Stanford's Department of Psychiatry and in private practice, he offered many insights into the psychology of the types that he had gleaned from working with clients for decades.

Opening myself to other Enneagram guides, I found Russ Hud-son's teachings to be clear and inspiring as I learned more about the triads of the types. Russ easily leans into the gifts of each type while reminding us of the delusions we live in, demonstrating a balance to his teaching.

In 2018, I became a student in the Diamond Approach (founded by Hameed Ali, also known as A.H. Almaas). The Diamond Approach work gives me the courage to go deeper into my own pat-terns, into my inner scariness and beauty. Sandra Maitri is a senior teacher in my group, and her presence and wisdom offer me a model of centeredness, transparency, and compassion. Sandra is a master-ful teacher of the Enneagram System, and her books *The Spiritual*

Dimension of the Enneagram and *The Enneagram of Passions and Virtues* have been invaluable in helping me understand the deeper dimensions of my Enneagram type and all types.

These teachers, in sharing their knowledge and their presence, became the foundation of my Enneagram learning. I am grateful to each. Based on this foundation and over two decades of teaching and continued learning, I share my own perspective on this system. My understanding of the Enneagram continues to evolve as I continue to grow.

Accompanying my Enneagram teaching and learning is my spirituality, my life's priority. Three years in theology school at Emory University brought many gifts. Among those gifts were wonderful professors. Professor Roberta Bondi offered her knowledge of the Desert Fathers and Mothers (including Evagarius's Seven Deadly Sins) in ways that made the Abbas and Ammas come alive. Dr. Luther Smith, whose presence and prayers touched my heart, introduced me to the theology and spirituality of Dr. Howard Thurman, whose teachings and ideas shape how I speak about love. I seem to quote either Smith or Thurman weekly! Lastly, Dr. Thomas Thangaraj, a beloved teacher to many of us, gathered groups to travel to India and experience a non-tourist look at the people and the culture. My summer in India taught me that all is sacred, and I learned that I could live more simply. It took a few years for me to understand that these two qualities—simplicity and sacredness—are intimately connected.

What to Expect

Part One provides the foundation for the Enneagram type chapters in Part Two of the book. It begins with a discussion of and some reminders about presence. Presence is *the foundation for learning, growing, and relating*, and it's a gateway to moving beyond our type. Learning about our Enneagram type doesn't change us. Insights and new learnings are stimulating and fascinating, but not transformative. Insights from the Enneagram Map, when coupled with presence practices and inquiry, support transformation.

Questions for reflection and practices to support our becoming more embodied humans conclude the first chapter. Some of these suggested practices may seem odd. Give them your best effort for an extended period of time, and notice any shifts that may occur. Our practices and inquiry shape us into the humans we want to become.

Part One continues with foundational material about the Enneagram: what it is and is not. Exploring the numerous dimensions of the nine ego structures brings clarity to the "why" behind behaviors. This part of the book concludes with a discussion of the three centers of intelligence (body, heart, and head) as well as other Enneagram triads. I offer suggestions of practices for moving counter-instinctively to ego and triad patterns, invitations that provide entry points into different responses in difficult situations. Finally, I pose questions that allow access to all three of our "brains," expanding our curiosity and reducing our blind spots.

Part Two includes chapters specific to each type, organized according to the three centers of intelligence and beginning with the type at the center of each triad. The chapters start with an overview of the type and its inherent strengths, then explore the type's vice and virtue, fixation, and spiritual perspectives. In each chapter, two companion voices speak to the "inside story" of their Enneagram type, sharing patterns and narratives of their type and how they are moving beyond type and into their authentic selves. Their voices help the types become more visceral and alive.

For each type, I identify some **compassionate entry points** that others can draw upon in their interactions with this type to grow healthier relationships. I also provide suggestions for loosening the grip of the type through type-specific practices, journaling questions, and Sabbath-keeping ideas. These practices and reflective questions are sources for our liberation into our authenticity.

The power of the Enneagram Map lies in what it reveals about what makes us tick, and this knowledge guides us in shaping practices that pause automatic responses and return us to presence. In presence, when our type recedes, our virtues and spiritual perspectives come forward, reminding us who we really are. Truly, in these moments, we are radiant. We stand in the Essence of ourselves. If this is difficult to understand, then remember a time when you were in awe, startled by surprise into a beautiful and still moment. At such times, our Enneagram type dissolves. We are free of patterns that blind and bind us. We stand in the Oneness of the moment, expanded into the glory and beauty of ourselves.

In each type chapter, I refer to power in a particular way. When Ones are accepting, they stand in their power to be. The same is true for Sixes; when their power of trusting arises, Sixes embrace their power to be. I am not referring to the power "to be able to," such as the power to purchase, the power to win or to influence, but rather to the power to be fully who we are, to be ourselves without the confines of our Enneagram type. *That* is the power to be. This power has presence, heart, kindness, and strength. May we each grow into it as we move through our days.

Part Three illuminates that *resistance keeps us stuck, while allowing and receiving change us.* As quantum physics reminds us, "What we fight, we strengthen." This chapter introduces the PAUSE Process, a support for moving through an emotion that seems to have us hijacked and buckled up tightly into our type. Additionally, a discussion of converting the vice energy to the virtue provides a foothold for welcoming and accepting all of who we are. For all of us, this work moves us from righteous indignation into becoming more curious and compassionate participants in our world. A list of suggested resources follows Part Three, as well as biographical information on the contributing writers.

Poems and quotes from various authors and speakers are peppered throughout these chapters to give more dimensionality to the discussion of the Enneagram types. Questions for reflection and journaling as well as practices that go counter to our automatic patterns are included in each chapter. The importance of adding inquiry and practices to our Enneagram understanding cannot be overstated. Any transformation needs to be embodied, since patterns live in our bodies. A saying from the Asario Tribe of Indonesia and Papua New Guinea puts it best: "Knowledge is only a rumor until it lives in the muscle."[2]

Because we are more than our type, saying "I lead with type Eight" or "those who lead with type Eight" is more appropriate than "I'm an Eight" or "Eights." However, in this book I'll tend to simply name the types for the sake of simplicity. When I began to teach the Enneagram, it felt important to teach that we are more than our type. Our Enneagram type, or ego structure (I'll use these terms interchangeably), is our inner comfort zone of patterns and responses that support a familiar self: our ego's vision of the ideal self for us. The ego doesn't recognize the larger story of us, as it continues to believe that we are still young. We have a deeper Self, our Essence or Ground of Being. When we are present, we stand on this Ground and the smaller self of our ego/Enneagram type recedes.

As readers, you are invited to soften your preconceived notions and images of the nine types, so that an open mind and heart guide your reading. Remember, we humans are already whole, and we are more alike than different.

CHAPTER 1

Grounding in Presence

Over the years of learning from and teaching the Enneagram, I have come to understand my Enneagram type as a portal, a path into my Ground of Being, my Essence. Moving past the trailhead and walking the trail takes courage and trust, because this path is difficult. The further we travel, the more clearly we see our inner landscape, and fears arise. Our Enneagram type or ego structure, afraid of "losing us," has signs posted on the trail to encourage us to turn back to our familiar territory of type. These structures exist to protect us, and when we approach the portal they go into overdrive, "protecting us" from the unknown. We hear inner messages: *I'll disappear! I'll change and others won't like me!*

Yet, grow we must. So, we take the next step of getting curious about our current experience. We observe our type operating, and we decide not to express the automatic pattern or believe the false narrative. Moving toward the portal isn't the same as living in the experience of our type. We see our type as a portal when we are in a state of presence and inner awareness. When we discover ourselves moving toward this portal, our greatest resource and support is our body. Our body is the container for the inner alchemy that allows us to move beyond our type. In this context, *alchemy* refers to our transformation of vice to virtue, fixation to enlightened spiritual perspective, automatic patterns to living with awareness, and to the shift from fear to love.

Given this understanding, we approach our study of the Enneagram with a discussion of presence. Without presence, we have no spiritual life. Being present to ourselves is the starting point. We are available to ourselves and able to observe ourselves when we are present in this moment. Transformation relies on our witness of ourselves. Next, we become receptive, allowing all the centers of intelligence to become accessible. Present plus receptive allows the arising of presence. We can make this happen. We relax into the moment in receptivity, and this opens the door to presence. Presence dissolves patterns and false inner narratives. Free of these habits and narratives, we can live in our own radiance. Presence brings a reverence to our living.

Grounding in the Land

I grew up in rural North Carolina, with lots of land to roam. Oak trees and White Pines offered their stately presence on the property, and vegetable gardens provided much of our food in the summertime and beyond. And, for a short time in my adolescent years, I had horses to ride. The outdoors was as much home as the house I lived in. My relationship with the land steadied me; the horses delighted me and played a key role in getting me solidly in my body. I felt my body relax and expand when I was outdoors, whether lying on the ground or sitting on a horse. In these particular moments, I knew in my marrow that I was held and that I was a part of creation. I became more present to myself and to my body's sensations. I still remember the smell of my colt's neck, the feel of the landscape underneath me, the peace of those times.

Through and with creation and creature, I was more available to myself. Instinctively, I knew at a young age that the land, the trees, and the plants were supportive, embracing me in their own way. As I've aged, I still lie on the ground when I'm lost to myself or confused, or I lean into a tree and feel its roots beneath me. I seek the wisdom and support of these rooted ones in times of discernment. I sit still and listen deeply. I am rarely disappointed.

We humans are a part of the natural world, yet we sense that we are separate from it more often than not. I believe this disconnect comes at a great cost. Eco-feminism teaches us that our healing and the healing of the Earth are connected. Tasks and technology, meetings and plans serve as barriers to our connection with the land. This separation may be one of the causes of our suffering. We sense that in some way we don't belong. Yet, when we hike into a forest, sit at the shoreline, climb to the mountaintop, we are restored. We find our place in the holy pulsing web of life and know that, yes, we belong and are worthy of belonging. Creation is diverse and all of it belongs; therefore, so do we. This knowing can lead us to honor the many parts of ourselves, the various perspectives among us, as well as the diversity of humanity. A rich life emerges when diversity is celebrated.

PRACTICES for Grounding with the Land

CONNECTING WITH THE EARTH

Locate a yard or field where you can lie on the ground and feel safe. Lie down for 10 minutes or longer. Feel the support of the Earth beneath you, holding you. Breathe deeply. From head to toe, relax into the Earth and offer gratefulness for her support. Notice your body's response to being held in this way.

Lying on the ground, fully landing in our bodies, allows the scattered pieces of ourselves to weave together. When life is overwhelming or when we are experiencing a loss, this practice can be a balm for us.

LISTENING TO A ROOTED ONE

In times of discernment or when wisdom is needed, this practice can be helpful. My initial experience of this exercise was with a Pine tree in Western North Carolina. I assumed the exercise was about projection. It was not. The notes I wrote that afternoon as I listened sit by my desk, as they have for more than a decade. One note of wisdom the Pine tree offered was, "Being grounded in myself and in this moment is an act of caring for others because we're all connected." This wisdom continues to echo in me when I find myself over-doing in my care of others.

Here's the exercise: Select a bush, plant, or tree, or allow one to select you. You may want to have with you a notepad or journal. Sit close to it and imagine feeling its roots beneath you. When you're comfortably seated and present, ask the rooted one, "Tell me about your Essence." Move into stillness and deep listening. Stay with this for at least 30 minutes. Listen within, and be open to surprise.

Grounding in the Body

When fully present to ourselves, we make space to move into receptivity. Presence arises in this receptive state, and we discover a rhythm in life whose foundation is Oneness. We flow into the heartbeat of Life and know the world to be nondual. Many of us experience this in moments of awe when we are outdoors or when we are surprised by beauty. These moments startle us into a presence that expands us, softens us, and invites us to relax into the wholeness we are. In presence, the past fades, our three centers of intelligence open, and we see reality as it is, without the narrow filter of our Enneagram type. We feel solid. Our full knowing is accessible. Our body is the starting point for spiritual experience and is the container for our transformation. Embodiment is integral to our self-awareness and creates space for our inherent compassion to emerge. Over the years, I have been privileged to witness clients' transformations as they moved into full presence in themselves by staying focused and curious about their experience in the moment. The result of this process is self-compassion, which then flows outward. The final chapter of this book discusses this in more detail.

Our bodies prefer expansion and will naturally open and soften with deep breaths and with a focus on our physical sensations. My Enneagram mentor, Dr. Daniels, was fond of saying "An open heart requires a grounded presence." Presence gives us choice: live life on automatic or live life authentically. Choosing the path of automatic, we remain in the comfort zone of the same old egoic patterns. We are not grounded in ourselves, and thus we are unavailable to anyone, including ourselves. Choosing to step beyond our familiar patterns is a courageous act that liberates us from the egoic habits that bind us in fear and blind us to the abundance and love that surround us. Presence transforms us.

Free from the confines of our type's comfort zone, we create new movements, new thoughts, and new neural pathways that support our growth. This freedom carries us into the sacred pulse of life, allowing our life force to be in flow with what is. So, why would we not honor ourselves and the life around us by being present and choosing to live authentically?

In my witness of myself and others, I see that we have lack attacks. We fear we aren't enough, don't have enough, and a mindset of scarcity takes over. (We enter the gates of Scare-City!) Our ego always wants more. We become seduced by certainty or urgency or the lure of being seen in a certain way. We believe the illusions of our ego's false inner narratives that connect our worth to certain behaviors. As an example, for people who lead with type Two, a sense of worthiness can be related to being needed and affirmed by others. Helping is the preferred form of connecting, so Twos may over-engage with others to get a "hit" of worth. While this is a false notion of worth, it lessens the anxiety that arises when Twos aren't feeling needed or connected. For all of us, simply noticing how often we look at our cell phones indicates the grasping for connection.

For those who lead with type Eight, impact equals worth. The juiciness of "getting it done!" or "making it happen!" is irresistible to Eights. Anxiety arises when Eights believe the false inner narrative that value comes from impactful behavior. This anxiety drives a grasping to be impactful that can be wearing on others and lead to fatigue for Eights. Twos and Eights will seek to quickly fill a vacuum by helping and making things happen. This fast-forward movement rushes one past a present and authentic self.

Allowing anxiety and fear to move us brings us back into the egoic loop. We arrive in Scare-City once again. We grasp and cling to what is familiar: the coping strategies of our Enneagram type. Sticking to an opinion, a preconceived notion, or a pattern of any kind shrinks us. Then we live with blinders on and lose our larger perspective. However, we don't have to live in such a small world. *To shed our blinders and cease our grasping, we look to our body.* Once grounded in our bodies, we can observe our patterns and mental fixations.

Self-observation is possible when we are present and connect with our inner observer. This observer creates inner spaciousness, a pause that births choice. Thus begins the process of our transformation. Strengthening our ability to self-observe is crucial to this process. If I can't see myself or notice what I'm about to say or do, then I remain in my Enneagram type's automatic loops. The choice offered in the gift of a pause, made possible by our inner observer, can free us from the clutches of our comfort zone and shift us onto a new path of authenticity. Pausing has impacted my own life so much that I created a PAUSE Process, described in this book's final chapter.

Walking a new path is supported by intentionality and practice. Moving in a new direction that is counter to our type structure can feel disorienting at first. Anxiety arises to entice us to return to our habitual ways. To continue a new behavior and to shift life-denying behaviors requires some necessary supports. Our practices must be detailed and type-specific to move counter to the lockstep patterns of our Enneagram type.

PRACTICES for Grounding in the Body

While the following practices are simple and brief, repeated over time they support change in us. They soften mindless responses and shift us into presence. Each of these practices supports a greater awareness of our contracted or expanded state of being. This awareness is crucial to our work with the vice-to-virtue conversion discussed later in the book. In my spiritual companioning sessions, I use one or more of these practices to bring myself and the other into the present moment.

In her book *Erosion*, naturalist Terry Tempest Williams writes, "Our undoing is also our becoming."[1] May these practices assist both our undoing and our becoming.

CONTRACTION TO EXPANSION (DIS-EASE INTO EASE)

As you walk toward others or among others, notice if you are tight, tense, and contracted. If so, take three deep breaths into the belly, followed by a lengthy exhalation. Feel your feet on the ground, and wiggle your toes. For five seconds, be where your feet are, noticing the physical sensations of each foot. Relax your shoulders and drop your jaw for a moment. Once you feel present to yourself, continue on.

ANTIDOTE FOR OVERWHELM

This practice is highly counter-instinctive, and I have discovered that it seems to expand time.

When the thought arises that you have a scarcity of time and you feel anxiety rising, find a quiet place to sit still for three to four minutes. Feel the support of the chair beneath you, and lean your back into the chair to feel its support there. Instead of thinking about what is making you anxious, focus on your physical sensations—touch, smell, sound, sight, taste. Breathe and imagine your feet moving through the floorboards of the building and through the topsoil into the Earth. Root yourself. When you feel more grounded, continue with your work.

My experience with this practice has been magical. As a task-oriented type (types One, Three, and Eight), I can be hell-bent on moving from one task to the next—completing and moving on is an automatic response for my type. I can feel anxiety arise if I'm delayed from addressing the task. Yet, when I allow myself to feel the anxiety and breathe through it, I relax. When my body has expanded and I'm no longer believing my false inner narratives, then I get up and thoughtfully accomplish what is needed. All gets done, usually with time to spare. I can't recommend this enough.

ASKING FOR A KIND WORD

This is my "stoplight practice" that I engage in when I sit at a red light. Whatever the word that's offered is, I consider it for the day.

Take some deep breaths into the chest area. Place your hand over your heart space and ask your heart for a kind word for you. If the word you hear is not kind, it is not from your heart. Ask again and listen again. Allow yourself to be touched by your own heart. Stay with the word until you sense your body softening.

In working with this practice, I am amazed each time when I hear the kindness my heart offers me. It's quite touching. When I receive the word from my heart, I speak it to myself several times to allow it to permeate me. This practice reminds me that goodness is inherent in me. I remember hearing the word "tender" and realizing that I hadn't been kind to myself in a while. I slowed my pace, noticed negative self-talk, and began offering myself kindness. On rare occasions, I have received two or three words that are usually related in a phrase or are interrelated in ways that make sense to me.

As the Story Goes

A young adult visiting Europe for the first time decided to travel to several countries and visit old cemeteries, many of them on the land of monasteries. After days of walking and feeling the peace of the landscape, she was startled upon reaching one of those cemeteries to find that the engraving on each headstone was only a first name and a certain number of years, months, weeks, or days. The inscription on the first headstone she saw was "Joseph, 5 years, 7 months, 22 days." The next read "Paul, 3 years, 4 months, 2 weeks." And on it went. She wondered if she was in a cemetery for children and approached a monk to ask. "No, this isn't a children's cemetery," he said. "Each headstone gives the name of a deceased monk and the amount of time he was present to his life."

Grounding in Being

Once we become present, we can go deeper by relaxing into receptivity. A receptive state is rare for us. It can feel scary because we surrender control of outcomes or next actions. We release our need for predictability, to know ahead of time. Receptivity is an experience of deep trust in ourselves and in what unfolds as we wait in presence. We receive what is before us. When present and receptive, we stand in the landscape of spiritual experience. A presence arises. We expand, our hearts open, and our minds are clear.

Receptivity is invitational. It allows the other to be who they are and to show up more fully. And, in this state, we hear more deeply and see more clearly the reality before us. Rather than reaching for, we receive what is. The Indian poet and philosopher Rabindranath Tagore said, "Everything comes to us that belongs to us if we create the capacity to receive it." In receptivity, our Essence arises and we embody our greater Self. We are fully rooted in the Ground of our Being. This Essential Self is who we really are. Our Enneagram type fades as our Essence emerges. The more frequently we stand in our Essence, the more we know the Ground of Being within.

Being receptive takes practice. The previously mentioned exercise with a rooted one requires us to be receptive. No expectations, no agenda, no projections. Another exercise that supports receptivity is the following one, which can be a supportive daily practice.

PRACTICES for Grounding in Being

GRATEFULNESS EXERCISE

This exercise is not the typical gratitude practice. It has four steps:

1. Get grounded and present to yourself.

2. Consider something specific that has occurred on this particular day for which you're grateful. Name more than just "good weather today." Perhaps it was the moment a songbird awakened you this morning, or the kindness of a stranger. Whatever you choose, make it particular to this day.

3. Name something about your own being, not the doing, for which you're grateful.

4. Take a deep breath with a long exhalation, and sit in gratefulness without an object. In other words, you are not grateful "for" something or someone, you're sitting in gratefulness as it comes forth from your heart. You might imagine relaxing into a lap, resting in gratefulness. If you're able to sit in gratefulness, notice when your body relaxes and softens. This indicates you're moving into receptivity.

May we live with presence and an aliveness that honors ourselves and the life around us. The world is more beautiful and our lives richer when we are present to ourselves and to the Earth and live from our Essence.

CHAPTER 2

Enneagram Basics—
The Inner Landscape

Understanding the interlocking aspects of our Enneagram type can provide us with insights into our own selves and compassionate entry points for engaging with others. Therapists, spiritual directors, and coaches may also find this information useful in getting to the heart of the matter for clients who know their type. Before we get into the specifics of the types, however, let's explore the foundations of the system itself.

The Enneagram symbol is ancient. The Enneagram Personality System is not. The symbol of the Enneagram can be found in explorations of sacred geometry dating back to Pythagoras. The 20th-century spiritual teacher G.I. Gurdjieff brought the symbol into the public sphere and used it to address questions of universal law and human consciousness. Bolivian philosopher Oscar Ichazo created the personality system in the 1950s and '60s. His student, Chilean psychiatrist Claudio Naranjo, made additional contributions to the system. To learn more about the origins of the Enneagram, I recommend reading Russ Hudson's foreword in A.H. Almaas's book *Keys to the Enneagram.*

All types are equal, all with challenges and gifts. *No type is better or worse than other types.* We remain the same Enneagram type throughout our lives. Behaviors soften and change. Our Enneagram type, or ego structure, is a constant, supporting us as well as derailing us.

We all have a bit of all nine types in us. While one type is our default, our home base and the one we lead with, our resource points have an influence on our type. The resource points are our wings and connecting types. The wings are the types on either side of us. One of these can flavor our type more than the other. I have found that around midlife, our stronger wing may shift. Life seems to want to balance us. Recognizing and implementing the *gifts of both of our wings* is part of our work. The connecting points, those types that connect to us by lines on the Enneagram symbol, have a key role in who we are and how we navigate our lives. I encourage readers to understand as fully as possible their lead type, then begin the study of these two connecting points. We have some attributes of the remaining four types too. Our path is to integrate the perspectives and gifts of all nine types.

Nature and nurture create our Enneagram type (ego structure). The Enneagram is a complex map of our internal operating system. Some neural preferences seem to be with us at birth, including the wiring of our nervous system, our information filters, and our particular physical energy. Mental health professionals agree that our preferences and automatic patterns are in place by the age of five to seven. Recognizing these patterns and how they move us is a starting point on our path toward authentic living. The Enneagram is *more than a typing system.* Discerning our type is the beginning point of working with the Enneagram Map, not the end point.

The Enneagram dives beneath behaviors, revealing our motivations, focuses of attention, mental frameworks, core fears, and natural strengths. *It is not a description of behaviors.* The culture in which we were raised, socioeconomics, and our family system helped to shape our behaviors. While a type One in Singapore and a type One in Boston will process information similarly, their behaviors will be different because of cultural experiences and expectations. Likewise, whether we grew up with financial means or without them shapes our behavior. Our Enneagram type is deeper than our behaviors.

The Enneagram indicates preferences. *It does not predict how we will think or behave.* We humans will continue to surprise ourselves. A posture of curiosity and openness allows us to see the person, not the type.

The Enneagram liberates us from limiting patterns. *It is not a system that pigeonholes or confines us* to a type box. The Enneagram Map shows the complexity of our inner limiting patterns that deny us our full dimensionality. Working with the map and implementing particular strategies and practices supports us in moving beyond automatic patterns and the limitations of our type.

Each of us is a unique expression of our Enneagram type. *There is no poster child for each type.* Knowing someone who leads with type Three doesn't mean that other Threes will behave like the person you know. Just because you have two friends who lead with type Four who behave similarly, it doesn't mean all Fours behave as they do. So, rather than thinking, "Oh, you lead with Six. I know about you!" instead we might think, "Oh, you lead with Six. I wonder what I'll learn about your unique expression of this type."

Self-exploration and self-observation are crucial to discerning our Enneagram type. Online tests can short circuit our exploration. And, it's best not to type others. Assessing our type is an inside job, since the Enneagram isn't about behaviors. Many types have similar behaviors. For example, both Ones and Threes are driven to complete tasks. Both Sevens and Twos can be positive, kind, and enthusiastic. Our quest is to learn the "why" of these behaviors.

Our type can be used as a portal to our Essence. When we get present and dig into our type's vice or fixation or ego ideal, we can move through the patterns and false narratives and arrive in our Essence.

The Enneagram is a psychospiritual system. We are more than our Enneagram type. *The Essence of us, our Ground of Being, is who we are.* This deeper Self comes forward when we are in presence. Then, our type recedes. Frankly, we do not want to be our Enneagram type, because our type is a set of automatic patterns and false inner narratives that narrow our perspective and close us to our hearts. Working with the Enneagram Map supports deepening our self-awareness, the first step in connecting with our Essence. Living with presence and mindfulness opens us to our Essential Selves. If we continue to be unaware of those false narratives and knee-jerk reactions to life, we will spend a lifetime in lockstep with our automatic patterns, and we will miss out on our lives! When present to ourselves, we expand and open to our hearts. Compassion arises. We see reality as it is through our enlightened spiritual perspective (Holy Idea). We recognize our lives as sacred. We know that we belong to the sacred and intimate pulsing web of life.

Given this basic information, let's explore some of the key inner workings of each type's makeup that keep us on automatic. Keep in mind that this is a toe in the water of this complex system. This discussion focuses on some key components, not the entirety of our ego structure. None of these pieces is a lone operator. Each plays a role in the makeup of our ego structure's efforts to protect us as it did when we were young. Our ego doesn't know how old we are! It continues to operate as if we were five, six, or seven years old. We need this structure to survive in our world, and it has numerous gifts. And as we become more aware of how our ego operates in our lives and moves us, we can choose to continue in its patterns or not. The Enneagram Map is a tool to deepen our awareness of our inner workings so we can move beyond our type. Waking up to our lives is a deep honoring of ourselves.

The Ego Ideal

Keep in mind that I use "Enneagram type" and "ego structure" interchangeably.

Each of us buys into certain stories about ourselves that our ego structure constantly feeds. While supporting these storylines, the ego simultaneously steers us away from parts of reality and parts of ourselves that would contradict these stories. The foundational story, the one from which other storylines flow, is the idealized self, or the ego's ideal version of us. This self is only a part of who we are, but at times we may believe it's all of who we are. This belief limits us and denies us our full dimensionality.

When asked what we like about ourselves or to name some of our gifts, usually we draw from our ego ideal. As one who leads with type Eight, my idealized self is "I am strong and make an impact." While there is some truth to this, it is only a fraction of who I am. From this idealized self, other stories form, such as "I am autonomous." If I inquire into this identity, another story may arise telling me that I don't belong and that I'm rejected, and therefore I need to be autonomous. "It's all up to me!" Inquiring further, I hear the inner whispers that I am bad. Those who lead with Eight will feel resonance with these identities, these inner stories. Remember that these are false stories.

The ego's ideal story of us sooner or later becomes a major part of our identity, and our automatic patterns work to maintain this identity. Without inner exploration, the ego ideal holds us captive, stunting our growth. The more we learn about our inner workings and engage in practices that counter our patterns, the more often we can experience our wholeness.

From years of working with individuals and organizations and leading Enneagram type panels in workshops, I've learned to ask, "Who are you beyond your ego ideal?" The responses commonly refer to the opposite of the ego ideal. For instance, when asking a type One "Who are you beyond your ego ideal of 'I am responsible and good'?" I often get replies like "Well, I don't want to be lazy!" Such a response comes from the ego working to maintain its ideal story of us. It purports that the opposite or the extreme is likely to occur if the ego ideal is challenged, in order to keep the ego ideal in place. Naturally, Ones don't want to be lazy. It's an easy sell by our ego! **Dualities are the domain of the ego.** The more extreme the duality, the tighter the ego's grip on us. In such conversations, I might ask, "What's between responsible and lazy? Where is the holy middle ground between these polarities?" For Ones, perhaps "relaxed" is easier to approach than lazy. And can Ones be responsible and relaxed, even lazy? Yes! Polarities are held in unity; all is a part of the whole. So, embracing *both/and* thinking is important work in softening the grip of our storyline. In this softening, we begin to shift our identity and realize that we are more than we believe ourselves to be.

While we all have many such dualities in us, one of the predominant dualities of each of the nine types is described below, starting with the body types, then moving to the heart types and the head types:

Type Nine: The duality of *accommodate or resist* suppresses a present self, a self that claims who I am and what I want and need. When present to themselves, Nines can honor others' wants and needs as well as their own.

Type Eight: The duality of *passionate or indifferent* denies simple, curious engagement that is neither for nor against.

Type One: The duality of *right or wrong* moves Ones away from accepting what is while naming "different" as wrong. Acknowledging a middle ground allows more than one right way.

Type Three: The duality of *accomplished or unimpressive* creates a blindness to the genuine Beingness that is held in the efforts and embrace of all.

Type Two: The duality of *approval or rejection* creates a blind spot for self-care and receiving support from others, which can restore Twos to relationship with the self.

Type Four: The duality of *ordinary or extraordinary* creates a blindness to the depth and simplicity that a steady calm offers.

Type Six: The duality of *certain or uncertain* creates a blind spot for trusting what unfolds and denies the Faith that arises in trusting the next step.

Type Five: The duality of *boundaries or depletion* creates a blindness to abundance and gratefulness. Having more than enough is a foreign concept to most Fives.

Type Seven: The duality of *options or limitations* create a blindness to the richness and freedom of this moment, right here, right now.

Our bodies help us notice when our false stories are operating and the behaviors these stories support. Over-doing, over-engaging, and, for some types, withdrawing are clues that the ego ideal is activated. Making space for both/and relaxes the story and frees us a bit from the suffering we experience when over-identified with our ego ideal. A grounded body and open heart support this process.

A dominant **ego ideal** for each type is:

Type Nine: I am peaceful and settled.

Type Eight: I am strong.

Type One: I am responsible and good.

Type Three: I am accomplished.

Type Two: I am connected and helpful.

Type Four: I am unique, different.

Type Six: I am loyal and connected.

Type Five: I am knowledgeable.

Type Seven: I am upbeat and positive.

The ego has a need for more, and our "striving for more" is a clue that we've lost ourselves to our automatic patterns. When holding on tightly to this small version of ourselves, we make great efforts to be more helpful (Twos), more knowledgeable (Fives), etc. This striving and holding on shrinks us. When we consider ourselves to be more than this ego ideal, we begin to stretch toward our fullness. "Yes, I can be peaceful and settled as one who leads with Nine, *and* I can claim my voice and offer my opinions!" The ego ideal is a mimic of our Holy Idea, and when we get locked into striving to maintain this ideal, we distance ourselves from our Essence.

Bringing Awareness to Your Type's Core Issues

INQUIRY

+ *How do you behave when the ego ideal is in play? What do you sacrifice in order to maintain your ego ideal?*

+ *What is your felt sense of your ego ideal? How does it move your body?*
+ *What does your ego ideal protect you from? Who are you beyond this ideal? When you consider this last question, notice if your mind creates a duality.*

Continuing our inner exploration, the synergy of these components of our Enneagram type demonstrates the complex weaving of our remarkable Enneagram type structure.

The Focus of Attention and Motivation

Our type's placement of attention powerfully pulls our energy toward the object of its focus. This focus of attention is always with us and narrows our perception, especially in times of stress. During workplace crunch times or tangles in intimate relationships, this focus shapes what we see in subtle and not so subtle ways. Our focus of attention props up the ego ideal and works to sustain the motivation that drives behavior (see diagram A at the end of this chapter). It also limits our seeing. This blind spot is the opposite of where we focus our attention. When someone who leads with type Four focuses on "what is missing," it can reveal ways to be unique. Whether it's how a Four teaches a topic that isn't taught, preaches an uncommon sermon, acknowledges emotion, or offers a unique leadership style, this focus is a driver. Longing is a result of focusing on what is missing. What goes unnoticed is what is present that Fours appreciate.

I appreciate this quote from Gurdjieff student Jeanne de Salzmann: "The question is not what to do but how to see."[1] Yes, *energy follows attention.*

The **focus of attention** and **motivation** for each type are:

Type Nine: *Others' agendas*—this supports the motivation *to maintain harmony.*

Type Eight: *What is out of control*—this supports the motivation *to protect self and others from vulnerability.*

Type One: *Disorder or error*—this supports the motivation *to improve.*

Type Three: *Tasks to do*—this supports the motivation *to accomplish and be recognized.*

Type Two: *Others' needs*—this supports the motivation *to receive approval and be affirmed.*

Type Four: *What is missing*—this supports the motivation *to long for what was or could be.*

Type Six: *The worst case*—this supports the motivation *to anticipate harm and be safe.*

Type Five: *Detaching and observing for possible intrusions or demands*—this supports the motivation *to maintain privacy and boundaries.*

Type Seven: *The best case*—this supports the motivation *to be stimulated.*

Knowing where our type first directs our attention is one of the Enneagram's great gifts. **What we scan for, we will find.** Our type structure will channel our focus of attention to that which supports its patterns and motivation, while blinding us to the opposite of this focus. Using type Six as an example, the Six's focus is on worst-case possibilities with a motivation to stay safe. Noticing when this focus is in play, Sixes can then expand their focus to include their blind spot of best-case possibilities or to scan for people and situations that are safe and welcoming. Sixes may experience lessened anxiety when they expand their focus. We uncover some of our blind spots when we look in the direction opposite from our customary pattern.

Connecting the focus to the ego ideal is obvious. Staying with type Six's worst-case thinking, we see how being "loyal and connected" can create a sense of safety for Sixes if the worst really happens. If trouble lies in wait, there is safety with others. A focus on tasks for type Three supports the ego ideal that "I am accomplished." In choosing to expand our placement of attention, we create some distance between ourselves and our ego's story of us. This choice grows us.

Another action with great potential to grow us is to ask ourselves who we are aside from our motivation. For Ones, "Who are you aside from your striving to improve?" Or for Fours, "Who would you be if nothing were missing and there was no need for longing?" Our responses to these kinds of questions serve to loosen the grip of our identification with our small selves, our limiting inner stories. "I am someone who improves," says the One. Yes, and who *else* are you?

Bringing Awareness to Your Type's Core Issues

INQUIRY

+ *When do you notice your focus of attention being most fixed and narrow? How does your body feel when your focus is fixed?*
+ *What allows you to expand your focus and include more of reality? How can your body support this?*
+ *Consider the perspectives of the other eight types. Which two perspectives might you add to your own to support more thoughtful decision making?*

♦ *How does the energy of your type's motivation feel in your body? If you lead with One, for example, how does the energy of improving shape or move you? Who are you beyond your driving motivation?*

PRACTICE

Our type's placement of attention shrinks how we see reality, so there is much we miss. *Consider looking for something besides your type's focus.* If you lead with Three, you have a focus on "tasks to do." You might shift your attention to relationships, bringing more attention to being than doing.

What do you want to see, or find, in your day or during the week? Specificity and intentionality are necessary for this practice. Be specific about what you want to see, then be intentional in reminding yourself to look for it. Notice any changes in your mood as that which you seek comes toward you.

The world is born anew when we *hit our internal refresh button* by shifting our attention. This isn't as easy as it sounds, but with repeated practice we can, in the moment, expand our view. Pause, get present with yourself, and shift your focus. Seeing with new eyes brings us to new landscapes without the need for cars or planes.

Joy is just a shift of attention away!

The (Unconscious) Worldview

Our unconscious worldview is a narrow understanding of how the world operates, and some of our inner assumptions emerge from this false view. It contracts us and engenders fear while strengthening our motivation.

The **unconscious worldview** for each type is:

Type Nine: *The world is neglectful and ignores me.* (I'll maintain harmony and remain hidden so I don't feel the pain of being neglected.)

Type Eight: *The world is a jungle that destroys the weak.* (So, I'll protect.)

Type One: *The world is chaotic and needs improving.* (I'd better start making it better.)

Type Three: *The world is a competitive arena where you win or lose.* (I'll be a winner.)

Type Two: *The world is full of interpersonal needs.* (Others need me to support them.)

Type Four: *The world is an abandoning place.* (Longing will keep me going.)

Type Six: *The world is dangerous and can't be trusted.* (Best to anticipate trouble.)

Type Five: *The world is demanding and depleting.* (I'd best pull back.)

Type Seven: *The world is limiting and confining.* (I'll keep moving so I don't miss out.)

Returning to type Six, if the world is dangerous and can't be trusted, then a Six might think, "Being connected and loyal can help to keep me safe." A Six's focus on worst-case scenarios, potential trouble, and emotional loss amplifies this worldview.

Over the years, I've found that crafting a counter-statement to my worldview—one that seems unbelievable—has been helpful in expanding my focus, softening my type's worldview, and reducing my anxiety. I am not suggesting creating an affirmation. Rather, *I use this counter-view to shift my attention so that I look for the unbelievable.*

Leading with type Eight, I experimented with rewriting my worldview from "The world is a jungle that destroys the weak" to "The world is supportive, and people want to be kind to me." I wanted to believe this statement, but initially it didn't hold merit for me. So, I dedicated myself to a three-month experiment. I repeated this statement to myself three times each day in order to shift my placement of attention and look for ways the world supported me. I looked for ways people were kind to me. I kept looking. By the third week, I was seeing some evidence for such a worldview. By the sixth week, I was beginning to believe it. At the end of the three-month period, I knew that kindness was abundant and was moving toward me. This change in my placement of attention brought a major shift in my inner belief system. My armor began to soften as I expanded my scan to look for ways I was carried. And, I found them! This experiment taught me that I don't need to expend so much effort.

Pausing here, I want to make the point that my particular crafted counter-worldview worked for *me*, given my type and my life experiences—childhood, culture, etc. Even if you lead with type Eight, this may not be an appropriate counter-view for you. Our personal life experiences give us our own unique understanding and expression of our type. People of the same type have unique life experiences that need to be honored and considered when creating practices and strategies. Again, this is not an affirmation, but rather a statement that reminds us to shift our placement of attention.

Bringing Awareness to Your Type's Core Issues

INQUIRY

* *What inner assumptions arise from your worldview? What statement might counter your worldview?*

PRACTICE

Imagine a new view of the world: one that is difficult to believe, yet possible. Repeat this description to yourself daily for two to three months, and shift your placement of attention. Notice any changes in your body. Is your worldview less believable? If so, how does this change you?

The Defense Mechanism

The defense mechanisms are covert operators! They can be difficult to recognize. However, we know they are in play when the ego ideal is consistent and strong. Diagram B at the end of this chapter indicates the defense mechanisms and core avoidances of the types.

Defense mechanisms defend. They guard against any evidence contrary to our ego ideal by shutting down emotions and sensations. Our ego structure is an exquisite design! When moving into a defended posture and over-identifying with the ego ideal, it's good to remember: *"Senses, not defenses!"* Noticing our sensations and taking some deep breaths supports us in returning to a broader perspective, one less identified with our ego's story of us.

The **defense mechanism** for each type is:

Type Nine: *Narcotization*—a dissociation that erases one's desires and tamps down energy. Sustains an image of a peaceful person.

Type Eight: *Denial*—inability to take in whatever indicates a lack of strength while hiding vulnerability. Maintains an image of strength.

Type One: *Reaction formation*—responding in a way that is opposite one's true feelings. Maintains an image of appropriate and good.

Type Three: *Identification*—identifying with success so fully that one's inner life takes a back seat. Maintains a winning image.

Type Two: *Repression*—tamping down one's own needs and whatever else is deemed "unsightly." Maintains an image of being saintly, helpful.

Type Four: *Introjection*—comparing what is real to an internal ideal (of self, other, or situation). Supports a need to be unique.

Type Six: *Projection*—attributing to others what one can't see or accept in oneself. Sustains loyalty to others.

Type Five: *Isolation of affect*—staying in one's head to maintain distance from emotions. Supports intellect.

Type Seven: *Rationalization*—reframing to the positive. Maintains the image of being okay and supports a mentality of "it's all good."

Consider the ego ideal of type Seven, "I am upbeat and positive." Exploring the workings of this Enneagram type, we find this ego ideal is supported and held in place by rationalization, the defense mechanism for Sevens. Rationalization is a reframing to the positive, no matter the difficulty. A focus on the "best case" solidifies this posture. When asked "What are you besides an upbeat and positive person?" a likely response from this type may be, "Well, I don't want to be a downer!" Here is the dualistic thinking of the ego again. What is the middle ground between being upbeat and being a downer? Understanding that, say, a part of me is sad and a part of me is enjoying the sunrise will support Sevens in accepting all of who they are.

At times, Sevens will project their own discomfort with sadness onto others and believe that if they show any semblance of sadness, others will see them as negative and therefore disconnect. Counteract such projection by checking out these assumptions with others. Noticing others' responses when you show sadness and remembering those responses provides a useful reality check. Often, Sevens believe their mission in life is to keep others upbeat. This, of course, isn't true and can be wearing both for the Seven and for others. Each of us is responsible for our own feelings. Yet, daily, we all buy into the believable illusions of our type.

Bringing Awareness to Your Type's Core Issues

INQUIRY

+ *When do you notice a lack of feelings and sensations? What situations bring this about? What would support you in accessing your feelings and sensations in these situations?*
+ *In what situations are you most able to feel your emotions and access your body's sensations?*

The Vice

Each Enneagram type has a vice that contributes to the core of suffering. Vices are emotional habits that constrict us and move us in familiar ways. When our bodies are contracted, more than likely we're in the grip of our type's vice. Depending on our type, the vice may drive us forward or pull us back. Knowing how the vice feels in our bodies and when and how it operates in our lives is a crucial step toward liberation from automatic reactions. This awareness allows us to create intentional strategies and practices for softening vice-driven behaviors as well as shifting the energy of the vice itself.

The **vice** of each type is:

Type Nine: *Lethargy*, which creates a laziness toward the self and fogginess around one's own desires and priorities.

Type Eight: *Lust*, which drives one to seek immediate satisfaction; a primal instinct for having a desire met *now*.

Type One: *Anger*, which drives the judgment that the world is not as it should be.

Type Three: *Deceit*, which drives the performance of a role and continues the doing.

Type Two: *Pride*, which drives one to maintain a posture of "knowing best," giving but not receiving.

Type Four: *Envy*, which engenders a comparing mind and finds that what is better or best is elsewhere.

Type Six: *Fear*, which supports an obedient posture or an attacking posture.

Type Five: *Avarice*, which drives one to hold on to all the resources necessary for self-reliance.

Type Seven: *Gluttony*, which feeds the monkey mind of ideas, options, and possibilities.

To explore how a type's vice operates, we'll use Nines as an example. The vice of lethargy makes it difficult for Nines to know their wants and priorities, much less to act on them. This vice creates an indifference in Nines, a passivity that prefers to accommodate rather than activate. They may substitute comfort for their own desires. Comfort brings a low-level energy, a "whatever" attitude that can deny curiosity and imagination. Following routines day after day can be a form of comfort, and Nines can sacrifice their own aliveness for the sake of this comfort. In this state, there is the delusion that "I'm avoiding conflict." However, having no opinion and offering minimal engagement can be an invitation for conflict! It seems that the more Nines avoid conflict, the larger it becomes later. As Nines fall asleep to themselves, they may notice that others are forgetting them too, as if the Nine doesn't matter. Lethargy is a withdrawing, sluggish energy. When this energy is coupled with a false belief that "If I show up, I may cause conflict," Nines may sink into despair. Keep in mind that despair or sadness may be a cover for anger.

Part Three discusses the vice-to-virtue energetic conversion, a process of allowing the energy of the vice to expand without expressing it or judging it. Staying present to this energy makes space for our virtue to arise. Indeed, the body is a container for alchemy.

Bringing Awareness to Your Type's Core Issues

INQUIRY

+ *Consider how your type's vice feels in your body. How does it move you? Does it drive you forward? Move you faster? Pull you back?*
+ *Can you name three ways your vice operates each day?*

The Fixation

Along with the emotional habit of the vice, each type has a mental habit, a fixation that creates rigidity in our thinking and a distorted view of reality. Like our vice, our fixation contracts our body as it shapes the present with the past, narrowing our perspective on reality. Diagram C at the end of this chapter indicates the fixations and vices of the types.

The **fixation** of each type (and its connection to the vice) is:

Type Nine: *Indolence,* which maintains ease and comfort, leading to an indifference to one's own priorities and desires (lethargy).

Type Eight: *Blame,* which creates dualities and brings forth strong opinions that support deciding and acting now (lust).

Type One: *Judging,* which brings in a mindset of how things "should" be, creates dualities, and fans the flame of anger.

Type Three: *Vanity,* which drives a focus on image and accomplishing, supporting the notion of a competent, separate doer (a key deception).

Type Two: *Flattery,* which supports the image of one who is sensitive and loving as it seduces others to draw closer. It accompanies a *helpful* stance, keeping pride alive.

Type Four: *Melancholy,* which heightens feelings of deficiency. This is a breeding ground for a comparing mind (envy).

Type Six: *Doubt,* which engenders anxiety and fear, serving to maintain mistrust.

Type Five: *Stinginess,* which arises from a false belief of "not enough." This mentality of scarcity supports holding on to resources (avarice).

Type Seven: *Planning,* which keeps the mind focused on future possibilities and *options,* feeding gluttony and neglecting the present.

Next, we'll turn our attention from our egoic self to the qualities of our Essence. Our Ground of Being, our True Nature or Essence, is always with us. In our Essence, we are expansive, grounded in our bodies, and we are open to our hearts. Our minds have clarity. Our virtue opens us, and the Holy Idea brings a sacred seeing.

The Virtue

Our virtue is our life force. It opens us to wonder and brings us into the present moment. Our open hearts invite the arising of our virtue. We experience our virtue in moments of awe, when we are present and receive the moment as it is. This receptivity isn't passive, but an active taking in of ourselves and our surroundings through an enlightened spiritual perspective (our Holy Idea). We know these moments to be reminders of the sacredness of our lives.

The **virtue** of each type is:

Type Nine: *Self-remembering,* or *right action* (action that supports the self and the spirit of aliveness).

Type Eight: *Innocence,* which offers an unguarded posture without opinions, inviting the wisdom and kindness of others.

Type One: *Serenity,* which makes room for acceptance, soothing the need to improve and calming the task-orientated drive to complete.

Type Three: *Honesty,* which reveals that we are loved with no need for doing or accomplishing. Being comes alive.

Type Two: *Humility,* which allows for boundaries, a balance of giving and receiving, without an inflated or deflated sense of self.

Type Four: *Equanimity,* which brings a mental and emotional evenness, calming the comparing mind.

Type Six: *Courage,* which supports the inner exploration that leads to the discovery of the Ground of one's own Being, giving rise to trust.

Type Five: *Non-attachment,* which dissolves the belief in scarcity and brings abundance and generosity to the fore.

Type Seven: *Constancy,* which brings an abiding presence and a capacity to focus and stay with in order to complete what has been started.

Bringing Awareness to Your Type's Core Issues

INQUIRY

+ *When in your virtue, what are your body's sensations? Describe yourself in your virtue.*

The Holy Idea

Diagram D at the end of this chapter indicates the Holy Idea and virtue of each type. While there is much more to learn about the Holy Ideas than what follows, I offer here some basic information.

Our Holy Idea is a fresh, clear, unobstructed view of reality in the moment, an enlightened spiritual perspective. We are present to what is arising. When we are in this perspective, there is no past or future. The present moment contains All. Our Holy Idea and Holy Virtue arise together and expand us. As previously mentioned, moments of awe can land us in a receptive state from which our Holy Virtue and Holy Idea emerge and a spiritual experience occurs. In these moments, we come into our Essence, our Ground of Being, and our personality recedes. These moments are holy and remind us that we are holy beings. We are not a type but a loving, compassionate presence, whole and at one with All.

At birth, we are a bundle of receptivity with a particular energy. Freshly arriving in this Earth School, we take in our environment, the shapes of objects and shades of light. We sense ourselves, knowing when we are wet and when we are hungry or hurting. Sensation is our first way of knowing. We receive the gaze of our parents or caregivers. We live moment by moment in a receptive state, present to what is, seeing reality without biases from our past. Slowly—as the days, weeks, months, then years go by—this receptivity recedes as a belief in a separate self comes to the fore. This is a natural and necessary process as our ego structure takes shape, weaving our neural preferences at birth with our early life experiences. All too soon, we have a limited view of ourselves. (This formation process is complex, and books and resources abound that teach the intricacies of these early years.)

Yet, within us is a pull toward our Essence, to that place where we know we aren't separate. We long to return. Of the nine Holy Ideas, our particular Holy Idea is the gateway to that return to Essence. Once we move through this gateway and expand into our enlightened spiritual perspective, the other eight Holy Ideas follow, as if they were a package. However, ours is the one we are most sensitive to, the one we least understand, and the one from which we most dissociate. It seems blurry to us. A Five may ask, "Describe once again what Holy Omniscience means?" Or a Four may inquire, "What exactly does Holy Source mean?" The Holy Idea seems within reach, yet just beyond our grasp. And when we go through our own narrow gate and really understand our Holy Idea, we become the teacher of it. We know it in our marrow. Fives teach and live Holy Omniscience as they receive the wisdom that arises in engagement with others. Sevens become the teachers of presence when entering into Holy Work. Ones offer a nonjudging acceptance in Holy Perfection. We are beautiful to behold when we stand on this Ground of our Being.

We cannot attempt to capture our Holy Idea. We cannot earn it or strive for it. Our Holy Idea can only be received. We can only relax into it. The more we strive toward it, the more it eludes us.

When we notice ourselves "striving toward," it's an indication that we are imitating our Holy Idea. Believing we'll be fulfilled if we strive hard enough, we move in lockstep with our type's patterns in an attempt to secure our Holy Idea. This striving distances us from our Essence.

As an example of striving, let's consider the Holy Idea for type Three: Hope. Holy Hope arises from knowing "I have a solid foundation within that connects me with all." The ego's imitation of hope is that of being someone who gets things accomplished, a separate doer of tasks: "I can get this done and do more." A Three's drive to accomplish, driven by the ego ideal, brings a sense of hope, however false this is. The more Threes strive to do more, the more distant they become from the Holy Hope that recognizes Threes' interconnectedness. Threes do not accomplish alone but are a part of the Whole. Vanity, the Three's fixation, heightens the need to be impressive in the accomplishing, while diminishing the Three's being. In receiving Holy Hope, a Three's posture shifts to allowing as their effort lessens.

Each type's ego ideal is an *imitation* of the **Holy Idea**. A brief description of this follows:

Type Nine: Striving to maintain ease and *harmony* imitates *Holy Love*. This imitation prevents Nines from knowing that they, too, are unconditionally loved. In receiving Holy Love, Nines remember themselves and know, without a doubt, that unconditional love is a given for them. This enlightened spiritual perspective brings an aliveness, supporting Nines in fully claiming themselves.

Type Eight: Dualistic thinking brings forth strong *opinions* that imitate *Holy Truth*. Yet, Holy Truth is the understanding of a nondual world, a knowing of our oneness. In this unity, the Eight's armor dissolves as tenderness emerges.

Type One: *Right* imitates the Holy Idea of *Holy Perfection*. The striving to be a good person and get things right distances Ones from understanding that there is perfection inherent in all things and in everyone. When Ones stand in Holy Perfection, the drive to do good ceases as Ones allow their goodness to flow from them. From this enlightened spiritual perspective, they see order in disorder.

Type Three: *Efficiency* imitates *Holy Hope.* However, Holy Hope is understanding that our Ground of Being works through us and is our foundation. No one lives in isolation. Each action affects all others. When Holy Hope is received, Threes' lovable Being radiates forth, as the need for efficiency recedes and emotions, empathy, and compassion are genuinely expressed.

Type Two: *Helpfulness* imitates *Holy Freedom,* as it seems Twos can offer and give what they want and when they want. A natural giving and receiving arise in Holy Freedom as Twos surrender to divine flow without an agenda. This shift from willful to willing offers Twos space to attend to their own needs. Worth becomes a given.

Type Four: *Melancholy* heightens the comparing mind (envy), bringing feelings of deficiency into the foreground. This supports the striving to stand out or to be unique, the imitation of *Holy Origin.* Being connected to Holy Source or Origin is a given; this is a connection that always was and will be, regardless of how ordinary or extraordinary one is. Simplicity is a clue that Fours have relaxed into the connection to Source as they become a pool of deep calm.

Type Six: *Certainty* imitates *Holy Faith* and drives the striving to know ahead of time. Predictability seems safer. In receiving Holy Faith, Sixes stand solidly on their inner Ground of Being, trusting themselves in life's unfolding, however certain or uncertain. From faith in self, a faith in others emerges.

Type Five: A fear of separateness and of scarcity drives the seeking of more *knowledge* and a withholding of resources. Information and knowledge imitate *Holy Omniscience.* However, Holy Omniscience isn't information, but wisdom gleaned in and from relationships.

Receiving their Holy Idea, Fives engage with life and know they are a part of the whole. Life is abundant.

Type Seven: Neglecting what is present, Sevens strive to get their needs met by generating numerous *options* of plans. This imitates *Holy Work*. As Sevens begin to trust in the present moment, they stop imposing their plan onto Holy Work. In this enlightened spiritual perspective, Sevens know they are a part of and carried by the Divine unfolding. A quiet heart arises, one that has no need for options.

Evolving Consciousness

We do love our Enneagram type, right? It's our comfort zone. Its patterns are familiar and feel safe to us. For instance, troubleshooting seems safe for Sixes. Intensity feels juicy to Fours and Eights. Planning is such fun for Sevens. The comfort of our type is a continual draw. Yet we know, as the bumper sticker reads, that "Growth happens outside our comfort zone." To grow, we must be willing to risk discomfort and disorientation, and be curious about possibilities beyond those familiar patterns.

Present to ourselves and disengaged from our type's patterns, we see the world as it is. Inhabiting our enlightened spiritual perspective, the other Holy Ideas flow. We stand in the power of faith, hope, and love as well as the power of wisdom, presence, oneness, freedom, and perfection, and in our connection to Source. We have all we need within us.

One of the greatest contributions we can make to our community and to our world is to engage in life through our enlightened spiritual perspective, where compassion and love flow and we stand in our Essence. May it be so.

taking control
to protect self and
others from vulnerability
*What is supportive and
doesn't need controlled*

others' agendas
to maintain harmony
Own Agenda

9

seeing error
to reform and improve
*Order and what is
working well*

8

1

best-case scenario
to be stimulated
*Difficulties that
may arise*

7

Focus of
Attention,
Motivation,
Blind Spot

others' needs
to be affirmed
Own Needs

2

worst-case scenario
to anticipate
potential harm
Positive possibilites

6

3

tasks to do
to accomplish
Beingness, Emotions

5

4

detaching & observing
to maintain boundaries
and privacy
Abundance in the world

seeing what is missing
to continue the juice of longing
Gratefulness for what is present

DIAGRAM A

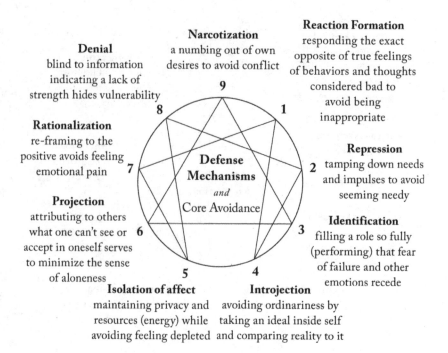

Reaction Formation
responding the exact opposite of true feelings of behaviors and thoughts considered bad to avoid being inappropriate

Narcotization
a numbing out of own desires to avoid conflict

Denial
blind to information indicating a lack of strength hides vulnerability

Rationalization
re-framing to the positive avoids feeling emotional pain

Repression
tamping down needs and impulses to avoid seeming needy

Defense
Mechanisms
and
Core Avoidance

Projection
attributing to others what one can't see or accept in oneself serves to minimize the sense of aloneness

Identification
filling a role so fully (performing) that fear of failure and other emotions recede

Isolation of affect
maintaining privacy and resources (energy) while avoiding feeling depleted

Introjection
avoiding ordinariness by taking an ideal inside self and comparing reality to it

9 8 1 7 2 6 3 5 4

DIAGRAM B

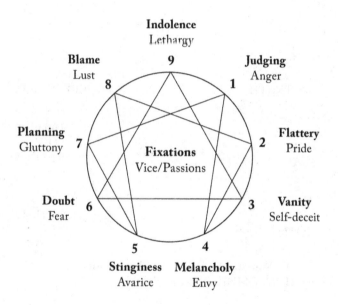

DIAGRAM C

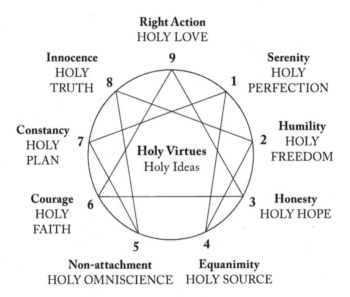

Right Action
HOLY LOVE

Innocence
HOLY
TRUTH

9

Serenity
HOLY
PERFECTION

8

1

Constancy
HOLY
PLAN

7

Holy Virtues
Holy Ideas

2

Humility
HOLY
FREEDOM

Courage
HOLY
FAITH

6

3

Honesty
HOLY HOPE

5

4

Non-attachment
HOLY OMNISCIENCE

Equanimity
HOLY SOURCE

DIAGRAM D

CHAPTER 3

Enneagram Triads

The Enneagram System includes numerous triads with different configurations of types. This chapter will discuss four triads. We'll start with the most important one, the three centers of intelligence. This is followed by a brief review of the Hornevian Triads, the Harmonics Triads, and the Enneagram of Harmony (Harmony Triads).

The Three Centers of Intelligence

The concept of the three centers was developed and taught by the Greek Armenian spiritual teacher G.I. Gurdjieff. He named these centers the *moving center* (body), the *emotion center* (heart), and the *cognitive center* (mind). Over the years, the Enneagram Personality System came to teach these centers differently from Gurdjieff. When working with the three centers of intelligence, I use the language of **sensing, feeling, and thinking** in expressing each center's first way of knowing.

The three centers, or "brains," relate to each other. When one center experiences a shift, the other two are impacted. The expressions "Move a muscle, change your mind" and "Shift your attention, change your mood" hold wisdom. Our full knowing arises when all three centers become accessible to us. Awareness of our body's sensations, as well as our emotional state, contributes to the clarity of our thinking and our experience of ourselves moment by moment.

The Body Center—Sensing

The body gives us our capacity to act, to be present. It's a truth teller. From the body center, we resource our rootedness and subtle ways of perceiving. Our capacity to act and decide is enhanced when we are present to ourselves. Noticing our physical sensations brings us into a direct experience of ourselves in the moment.

Instincts and physical sensations are first ways of knowing for the body types, Nine, Eight, and One. These types are fairness-oriented. Consciously or unconsciously, they are constantly scanning the environment for evidence of fairness or unfairness, in everything from public policies affecting all citizens to line-cutting at the movie theater. Injustice is a trigger for the primary emotion of anger. Additionally, anger arises when these types feel dismissed or unimportant. However, *when these types forget themselves, they believe the illusion that others are forgetting them. The work for each of these three types lies in remembering themselves rather than placing this responsibility of remembering onto others.* Forgetting the self takes several forms. Eights forget and project their fragility and fatigue, reaching out to support or protect an underdog or those they love. For Ones, desires and wants take a back seat to responsibilities and rules, especially in support of others. Nines prioritize others' agendas and forget their own priorities. Accommodating the requests and needs of others seems easier and is more likely to avoid conflict.

If you lead with one of these types, notice how anger drives your inner narratives or inner critic. "Just buck up! Be tough!" says the inner voice of Eights, impelling them to push aside tender feelings. Nines may hear "Don't make a big deal of yourself" or "This is going to be hard." These narratives nudge Nines to remain hidden. Most Ones can relate to the voice that says, "This isn't good enough. Do better!" Listening to this message, Ones work toward an A+ on all tasks, which is usually a futile endeavor. These inner narratives provide fuel for anger. When we become aware of these hurtful narratives, voicing a strong "OUCH!" is certainly appropriate.

While these "body" types are comfortable with and at ease in the body, oddly, they can be oblivious to their own bodies. Lacking awareness of fatigue or physical pain is a common way of forgetting the body. These types may delay medical attention, not realizing the implications of their discomfort. Physical self-care is an act of kindness. Engage in this practice of kindness!

The rhythmic motion of familiar routines brings comfort to body types. These types can be lulled to sleep in this comfort. While routines can be stabilizing, they can reduce body types to robotic behaviors, bringing a dullness to life. Cultivating imagination and curiosity about daily tasks supports mindful living and waking up to the inherent aliveness each of us possesses within.

For types Nine, Eight, and One, merging or counter-merging energies dominate. Both of these energies are barriers to the separate self, the self that is steady and stable and present. Matching the energy of others comes naturally for these types, which is both a gift and a curse. It can be a gift, as others see or feel that body types see them. For instance, I've experienced Eights downsizing themselves energetically when in the company of children. Appropriate in demeanor, Ones will shift their energy to synchronize with those around them. They "fit in." Examples abound to demonstrate the downside of merging, but one unique example shows up on the highway. While driving a car, I've noticed some Nines unconsciously matching the speed of the car they are following, speeding up or slowing down accordingly. There is a numbing out in merging energy. For all three types, this act of merging isn't conscious, and it takes some inner work and being present in order to maintain an awareness of self.

Counter-merging is the opposite of merging. Saying "no" quickly to another's request, idea, or invitation is an indication that counter-merging may be in play. While this may seem like evidence of having a separate self, it is simply an oppositional stance. The "no" is in response to another, rather than coming from a grounded presence and clear thinking. Body types will lack a clear perspective when engaging either of these energies, because they erase the authentic self.

Often, these types engage in dualistic thinking. Black-and-white thinking creates categories of right or wrong, your agenda or my agenda, with me or against me. In the background of these dualities is *fair or unfair*. Dualistic thinking, when coupled with gut instinct, gives rise to strong opinions and judgments. These birth a sense of certainty that shuts down curiosity and stifles imagination. Noticing when certainty is activated is a clue to begin asking more questions. While Ones and Eights may offer their strong opinions, Nines mostly pull back and nurse their certainty rather than expressing it. **Engaging curiosity** is a valuable practice for all three of the body types.

PRACTICES FOR BODY TYPES

+ To lessen self-forgetting, shake up daily routines. Use imagination and curiosity to consider other ways of moving through your days. Learn something new, drive home a different way, ask more questions. Create strategies for self-remembering each day.

+ When feeling certain, ask more questions! Certainty indicates a lack of presence.

+ Notice your body's fatigue level each day, and honor your body by resting and renewing. Engaging in playful or relaxing activities can be restorative.

+ Observe your relationship to boundaries. Are they too tight, or too permeable? Be intentional about setting boundaries. Give yourself more margin between tasks and meetings than you think you need.

✦ Accepting vulnerability is an act of inner strength and courage. Accessing and owning vulnerability allows movement to authenticity. For body types, this can mean feeling and naming sadness rather than expressing the anger that covers sadness.

The Heart Center—Feeling

From the heart center we find our passion, our courage, and the ability to attune to others. We consider what emotional quality is called for in situations and what emotion is arising within us. We are at ease with our emotional life. When we are open to our hearts, we can hold the creative tension between polarities and offer a discerning wisdom. The heart is the home of gratefulness, and from this feeling center we experience beauty and find our passion, our heart's desires.

Types Three, Two, and Four, the heart types, know first through feelings, mood, and tone. They are relationship-oriented, and their emotional intuition gauges the quality of their connection with others, feeling the emotional closeness or distance. These types can detect the mood in the room or of another and can alter themselves to mirror that tone or emotion. Also known as the image triad, they invest in presenting well to others. "How are you seeing me?" is an ongoing question within the minds of people who lead with these three types. They suppress themselves in order to become the image they perceive that others desire. A more useful question might be, "Who am I in my own eyes?" This question shifts one's worth from outside the self to within. These types sacrifice a faith in themselves or self-defined worth for the affirmation of others and to be seen in unique ways. Whether seeking to be the one who is most connected (Two), or most impressive (Three), or the one who uniquely stands out (Four), the cost of this quest for affirmation can be a lack of centeredness in the self. In putting forth an image, the authentic self is rejected for the sake of gaining worth in the eyes of another.

Altering themselves to get the desired attention and response from others is second nature for heart types. From this altering emerges a performance of themselves, crafted to elicit others' affirmation or applause. Emotions are coopted to play their role, so the presenting emotion may not be an authentic one. This performance may be conscious or may not be, but the body offers cues to discern between performance and authenticity. Performance is a posturing that freezes the breath and constricts the body. Authenticity lives in an expansive, relaxed body.

Heart types have an engaging energy that permits easy connection with others, and a natural social grace. An engaging energy can allow one to maintain an awareness of self while being sensitive to others. Engaging, however, can quickly shift to *over-engaging*, which emerges from a grasping to be connected and loved—to belong. Each of these types resonates with a sensitivity to being unlovable (an illusion commonly experienced by this triad) that drives their need to be affirmed and appreciated. My mentor, Dr. David Daniels, was known for asking heart types, "How would your behavior change if you didn't need another's approval or affirmation?" To this I add, "Who are you when your own approval is all you need?

The primary emotional issue experienced by the types in the heart triad is the shame or grief that arises when experiencing disconnection or rejection. Embarrassment is a clue that shame is just around the corner. If you lead with type Two, Three, or Four, notice when your inner narratives are shaming you. Twos may hear a voice saying, "You're useless." An inner voice in Threes may say "Failure is just around the corner, keep accomplishing," while Fours experience a shaming message that suggests "You're too much!" or "You're not enough." Remember, these are *false* narratives! You are loved, and you are worthy. And you belong. If this is difficult to believe, for a week, practice scanning for the ways you belong. Observing your relationships with family and friends as well as your relationship to the natural world can offer validation of your belonging.

When heart types believe their false inner narratives, grief may arise. In this moment, the invitation is to stay with this feeling. However, a common response from heart types is to reject the authenticity or the felt emotions of this moment and shift to performance. Self-rejection can be a subtle, low-level energy that drives these types to seek worth and lovability outside themselves. They project their own self-rejection onto others, and this projection sustains their performance. The more worth is sought from the other, the greater grief becomes. When heart types spend time in solitude, they often report that sadness bubbles quickly to the surface. In solitude, questions may arise: *Do others like or love my image or me? Am I loved for what I do rather than for who I am?* At the heart of these questions lies, *Do I love me?*

Heart types will benefit from exploring how they know, deep down, that they are worthy. Through self-inquiry, they may eventually discover that in seeking outside themselves to be defined as worthy, or successful, or uniquely qualified, they have abandoned themselves. This can be devastating, and it is necessary to acknowledge. When heart types see the ways they reject themselves, they can choose to turn inward; they can commit to themselves and regain their inner ground. Then, they can accept the love others are offering them. Over time and with continued self-observation and inquiry, a different person emerges: one who has learned, grown, and become more aware. Hallelujah! **Our worth is a given.** There is no need to earn it.

PRACTICES FOR HEART TYPES

+ Notice when you are performing an emotion and allow yourself to relax into your deeper feelings in the moment. What are your body's cues that you are performing? How does your body feel when you are authentic? When your "being" gets equal time to your "doing," authentic feelings become more important than impressing others.

+ Journal with the question, "Who am I outside of my roles?" What do you discover? While journaling, use a hand mirror to look into your own eyes (not at your face). What do you see in your eyes?

+ Spend time alone, preferably in the natural world. Stay with whatever emotions arise.

+ When you move toward another, be aware of your breathing, your feet on the ground, and your own emotional state. Notice the point at which you leave yourself and turn your complete focus toward the other. Work to lengthen the time you stay centered in yourself.

The Head Center—Thinking

Our head center gives us logic, reason, and analysis—the ability to see patterns in our lives and connect the dots of experiences and concepts. In this center, we access our imagination, which helps us to create options and possibilities. When grounded in our bodies, our thinking is clear, quick, and crisp.

The head types, Six, Five, and Seven, are logical thinkers who want to understand the "why" of a given situation. They automatically engage the brain first, where thinking, analyzing, planning, and processing rule. Known for their vivid imaginations and quick minds, these types are good problem solvers and tend to enjoy this activity. Being information-oriented, they are naturally curious. Learning and taking in more data are strong drives for these types, and emotions can take a back seat to this mental exploration. Information is seen as the vehicle for growth and change, but this desire to always seek more can disconnect them from heart-felt relating. Seduced by content, the feeling beneath the content goes unnoticed. A focus on facts can create a sense of dryness in these types as the connection to the heart center lessens. Information substitutes for emotion. Detaching occurs when the mind's focus on logic and analysis pulls energy up from the body into the head. In this moment, the head types may lose the ability to experience what the present moment offers.

An example of this that was shared with me was a type Six mother who noticed her habit of viewing all her children's performances through the screen of her cell phone as she filmed them to ensure she'd never lose the memory of the moment and to enable her to share them with grandparents. The need to be a good photographer interfered with her being present in real time: the two-dimensional space of the screen didn't convey the emotion of being present in three dimensions. She noticed the difference each time she looked up from the screen to make eye contact with her children, who would only then break out into a smile. The mind is engaged in framing the photo, but in this moment the heart's experience of the love between mother and child may go unnoticed.

Scanning the environment and taking in data to analyze and order is a barrier for landing in the experience of the moment. The inner world of the mind is rich, playful, and feels safe—so much so that processing may replace deciding and acting. The need for more information drives research and slows decision making. The head types like to know things "ahead of time," so they lean into the future to plan and anticipate and pre-think options and solutions. An underlying sensitivity to being seen as incompetent may drive the planning, need for predictability, and future-oriented thinking. While others don't see these types as incompetent, this inner narrative easily moves into the foreground of head types.

The primary emotion of fear arises when these types experience uncertainty and potential hazards. A strong need for safety and certainty drives future-tripping, leading to over-thinking and over-planning. This can muddle the mind and lessen clarity. A low-grade anxiety is common in these types, as inner narratives keep anxiety and fear alive. Fives may relate to messages suggesting, "You'll be depleted if you continue engaging." Believing this narrative, Fives fear a drain on their resources, so they detach. Thinking feels safer than relating. Those leading with Six can hesitate. Fear freezes Sixes, and "what if" narratives bring forth cautious behavior. For Sevens, fear propels them quickly to the "next" moment as they seek more stimulation. When Sevens believe inner narratives suggesting they are missing something, their calendars become overbooked, conversations are shortened, and their pace quickens. If you lead with one of these three types, occasionally checking in with yourself and asking "How is fear moving me?" can be a fruitful inquiry, helping you to learn and recognize more quickly the role of fear in shaping daily living.

When we live in fear, we can't hear our hearts. When we can't access our hearts, we report on our lives rather than reflecting on our living. Making a list of emotions can be an entry point into the classroom of feeling those emotions for head types. Remember, emotions give us information about who we are in this moment. Emotions need to be experienced within ourselves, not necessarily expressed (see Chapter 13 for more on this topic). As you read those last two sentences, notice if your inner thoughts went to "expressing emotions isn't safe" or "emotions are unpredictable." Our ego structure does its best to keep us in our comfort zone.

Life doesn't impact us or touch our hearts when we over-rely on thinking and remain disconnected from emotions and sensations. Focusing on emotions and sensations counters detaching energy by guiding us into our own embodiment. Exercising, getting out in the natural world, taking bubble baths, and dancing are just a few activities that bring us into our body. Clarity comes as we ground ourselves, open to our hearts, and engage a single focus in our mind.

PRACTICES FOR HEAD TYPES

+ Notice when you become future-oriented and begin to feel anxious. Practice coming back to this day, to this hour, and into your body in order to lessen feelings of overwhelm, doubt, and fear. There is no suffering in the present moment!
+ When over-thinking, go for a walk, run, or bike ride. Engage the body to bring energy from the head to the body.
+ Engage your five senses to support you in landing in your experience in the moment.
+ Notice when your inner narrative cautions you to hesitate and to fear being seen as incompetent. Breathe through this false narrative; ground yourself and embody a confident posture. Remain engaged with others and move forward.

PRACTICE for All Centers

This practice opens access to all three "brains."

Intentionally place your gaze on something or someone in proximity to you. As you gaze, notice what emotion arises, and notice your body's response. Continue observing and feeling the emotion that arises and the sensations of your body. Do you feel tight or relaxed? Light or heavy? Repeat this with a different object for your gaze. Notice when your heart opens and you sense that you land fully in your body. Be present to yourself for a full minute.

It may be helpful to remember the last time you noticed a hummingbird or a soaring bird of prey. What emotions did this evoke in you? What was your body's response? When I notice a hummingbird at my feeder, no matter how often it happens, I experience delight and joy, and my entire body feels lighter.

Weaving together these three centers of intelligence, we become **thoughtful and compassionate** participants in our world. Given our type, we know our lead center of intelligence, the one that is our natural go-to in problem solving and decision. Engaging this intelligence is a second nature. Explore the gifts and challenges of each center to support your discernment.

If the body center is your least used, practice relating to the world through the five senses. Sight, sound, taste, touch, and smell return us to our bodies. The body or sensing brain is least accessible to types Four, Five, and Nine.

If the heart center is your least used, make a habit of reading poetry and listening to string music (like adagios). Both are languages the heart can hear. The heart or feeling brain is least accessible to types Three, Seven, and Eight.

If the head center is your least used, bring more curiosity into your conversations and thinking. Ask more questions. Learn something new each day or each week. And practice adding "unless" to your vocabulary. The head or thinking brain is least accessible to types One, Two, and Six.

The Hornevian Triads

The Hornevian Triads are named after the psychiatrist Karen Horney and draw from her work that expanded Freud's theories about the different ways people manifest their desires in relational and social situations. These triads indicate how we behave to get our needs met: *flight (withdraw), fight (assert), or freeze (dutiful).*

The Flight or Withdrawing Types

Types Four, Five, and Nine work to get their needs met by stepping back and thinking things over. Thorough thinkers who consider long-range strategies and think multidimensionally, they have a "leaning back" posture in conversations with others as they deliberate over information. It can be difficult to know where they stand on issues.

For Growth, consider: How would leaning forward in conversations change your way of engaging?

Practice: The body is the repressed center for withdrawing types. Notice your body's sensations each day. At different times during the day, notice if you are more contracted or expanded. When you sit, sense the support your body has. Occasionally, lie on the ground and do the same.

The Fight or Assert Types

Asserting to get their needs met, types Three, Seven, and Eight make and implement decisions more quickly than others. They can take up lots of verbal as well as physical space and tend to lean forward in conversations. Thinking on their feet is a gift these types possess in times of transition, and they excel at getting things done.

For Growth, consider: What kind of engaging would give others more space? How would it feel to sit back and wait to speak?

Practice: The heart is the repressed center for assert types. To cultivate more access to the heart, read poetry, and pause each day to notice and feel the emotions that are arising. Slow your pace, feel your care for the people and places you love. Notice what touches your heart.

The Freeze or Dutiful Types

Asking questions is a way of getting their needs met for types One, Two, and Six. They are most dutiful to the critical superego voice, which can bring about a rigidity in thinking. They often hear the "shoulds" of life. While asking questions and considering best practices for actions are commendable, these types can become paralyzed by considering the implications of their decisions, unable to take the next step. In decision making, they are sensitive to the needs of others.

For Growth, consider: What would support you in seeing a larger context? How might you create "good enough for now" thinking, knowing that change can occur in the future?

Practice: The head is the repressed center for the dutiful types. Rigid "should" thinking and over-thinking cloud clarity. Exercise lowers energy into the body, helping the mind to clear. Practice softening your body. Relax your shoulders and jaw. Look out a window and gaze up and beyond the horizon to support a larger field of vision. Both of these actions can support more flexible thinking. Engage in activities that cultivate mental agility. Consider many options in problem solving.

The Harmonics Triads

When we are thwarted in getting our needs met, our behavior shifts. As a trained community mediator, I have found the Harmonics Triads to be useful in structuring the mediation container and process, so I will present them through this lens. These triads indicate how each type responds to the disappointment of not getting what we want, and how we engage with conflict: *reframing, containing, or expressing*.

The Reframing Triad: Types Two, Seven, and Nine

When faced with difficult situations or conflict, these types attempt to reframe things positively. In mediation, they look for positive outcomes.

For Growth, consider: Engage in rational thinking. Consider difficulties that may arise and impacts. Be careful not to overlook the problem!

The Containing Triad: Types One, Three, and Five

Thinking rationally helps to create order in processing information. In mediation, these types want a fair, safe, and ordered process.

For Growth, consider: Insert several pauses throughout the day so you can notice and honor emotions that arise.

The Expressing Triad: Types Four, Six, and Eight

These types engage with intensity. Type Four has an emotional intensity, Six an intensity of the mind, and Eight a physical intensity. In mediation, these types want all emotions and concerns on the table.

For Growth, consider: Engage in thoughtful silence and consider positive outcomes. Bring in whimsy.

The Enneagram of Harmony

The Enneagram of Harmony, or the Harmony Triads, is another grouping within the Enneagram System. As taught by Dr. Daniels (*https://drdaviddaniels.com/articles/triads/*), the Harmony Groups are broken down into *idealists, pragmatists, and relationists.* The Harmony Triads connect the nine types in new ways by including in each group a type from each centers of intelligence triad, Hornevian Triad, and Harmonics Triad, harmonizing the energies from the three triads. In other words, each Harmony Triad includes a body type, a heart type, and a head type; an asserting type, a withdrawing type, and a dutiful type; and a reframing type, a containing type, and an expressing type. Enneagram teachers Don Riso and Russ Hudson used different names for the Harmony Triads: Frustration (for idealists), Attachment (for pragmatists), and Rejection (for relationists).

The Idealists

Types One, Four, and Seven—the idealists, or utopians—hold on to a vision of the way the world could be in order to create life-giving environments and support the flourishing of All. These types tend to be innovative thinkers and can easily generate ideas and new directions. As idealists with a vision of utopia, they can experience frustration that reality doesn't measure up to the ideal or standard they long for—thus, Riso and Hudson's name of *Frustration Triad.*

For Growth, consider: Practice reverence for what is in each moment.

The Relationists

Types Two, Five, and Eight—the relationists, or the "power triad"— provide the power or charge for moving relationships or projects forward. They demonstrate different ways of working with energy in relationships; for instance, Twos move toward others to meet needs, Fives move away from others to offer facts and information, and Eights speak out to name what is required in a given moment, often moving against others. These types will see or feel rejection when rejection may not be a part of reality in the moment. They are *rejection-sensitive*, as Riso and Hudson have indicated.

For Growth, consider: Notice when and how you reject yourself. This is helpful in lessening the projection that others are rejecting you.

The Pragmatists

Types Three, Six, and Nine—the pragmatists—sustain systems and operations. Nines create harmony and are inclusive. Threes enable efficient functioning, while Sixes offer their collaborative skills along with insightful questions. Because these types tend to gauge how each person is relating to them, Riso and Hudson call them the *Attachment Triad*. Maintaining connections is a priority for those in this triad.

For Growth, consider: Think about how abandoning yourself plays a role in your life. Explore how your wants take a back seat to being seen well in the eyes of others (Threes), being more loyal to others than to yourself (Sixes), and valuing others' agendas more than your own (Nines). These are traits of abandoning the self.

PRACTICE for All Types

Samuel Lewis, the founder of Dances of Universal Peace, suggested in his book *Spiritual Dance and Walk* that if we can change how we walk, we can change our lives.[1] Authors of spy novels often suggest that to identify a spy who is in disguise, one must notice the way they walk. How we move our bodies tends to be consistent. Our Enneagram type moves us in particular ways, whether it's asserting, sauntering, or stutter stepping. By type, we have a particular energy. When I was almost five years old, my mother gave birth to twin daughters. In the crib, their energies were very different. One was very active, frequently moving her limbs, while the other was more passive and leaning on her. To this day, that energy tells me who is walking down the hallway before I see them!

Practice moving your body in different ways.

Play with different postures and body movements to see how this shifts your thoughts as well as your focus of attention. If you walk quickly, try a slower pace. Do you see the world differently when you do this? If you are someone who doesn't take up much physical space, try sprawling a bit. Notice what inner narratives arise. If you usually lean forward in conversations, try sitting back in your chair. Imagine you have Velcro between your shoulder blades, and stick yourself to the back of your chair. What is this like for you? Or, if you usually sit back, try leaning forward. What does this offer you?

PART TWO

The Nine Enneagram Types and Companion Voices

Body Types
Nine, Eight, One

First Way of Knowing: Physical sensation, gut instinct

Primary Emotional Issue: Anger

Orientation: Fairness

Energy: Merging or counter-merging

Sensitivity: Being dismissed, seen as unimportant

Growth: Cultivating more curiosity

CHAPTER 4

The Power of Claiming: Type Nine

At the top of the Enneagram, type Nine's transformation from self-forgetting to self-remembering is foundational to us all. Because we all have a little Nine within us, it's important to consider the ways we forget ourselves as well as what supports our self-remembering. In preparation for reading this chapter, connect with the Nine within you.

TYPE NINE AT A GLANCE

Strengths: Inclusive, approachable, can see and validate numerous viewpoints

Ego Ideal: I am peaceful and settled.

Focus of Attention: Others' agendas

Motivation: To maintain harmony

Worldview: The world is neglectful and ignores me.

Fixation: Indolence

Vice: Lethargy, self-forgetting

Holy Idea: Holy Love

Virtue: Right action or self-remembering

Brief Overview

Nines have an easy and accepting presence, inviting others to approach and engage. They get along well with people, easily finding common ground and validating different viewpoints. Their steady and calm demeanor feels supportive to others. When present, Nines are exceptional listeners! They are thorough thinkers who take time to consider multiple dimensions of a decision. When Nines have time to think through plans, problems, and projects, they offer great clarity that brings understanding.

This Enneagram type is the most self-forgetting, easily merging with the energy of others. This merging energy, along with a focus on others' agendas, makes it easy for Nines to be distracted by the pull of others' requests and demands. In these moments, they forget the most essential tasks and priorities. When not present to themselves, boundaries dissolve and feelings of overwhelm arise. Anxiety may quickly follow. Alone time is good medicine, as solitude provides the space needed for Nines to return to themselves and reestablish boundaries. With no other to merge with, their own agendas, desires, and priorities surface. They get clarity.

Counter-merging shows up when Nines feel controlled, rushed, or dismissed. When stubbornness arises and "no" is a constant response, the counter-merge has arrived. This may manifest as waiting/inaction and indecision. Waiting indicates a "no." When Nines say "maybe," this is likely also a "no"! Neither the merge with another nor the pushing back of the counter-merge comes from a grounded self. Inaction, going along, and pushing back are all invitations to turn inward, explore the emotions driving these energies, and inquire, "What do I want?"

Along with the energy of merging, the Nine's vice of lethargy is a self-forgetting. It creates a laziness or indifference toward the self. This is not to say that Nines are lazy people; on the contrary, they are productive, creative, and often take strong stands on social justice issues. Yet, in their personal lives, a kind of brain fog can set in. Seeking comfort in routines deadens aliveness. Lethargy keeps the attention away from oneself and on others, with all energy expended in support of others' happiness. A **compassionate entry point** is asking Nines what they want and giving them time to think on it.

The Striving and the Avoidance

One of the drivers of focusing attention on others' agendas is Nines' value of harmony. They strive to maintain a peaceful existence and avoid conflict. However, when overly prized, harmony is costly. It can silence. Much is sacrificed for the sake of getting along. The more Nines seek peace, the more they sacrifice themselves to accommodating and acquiescing. Honesty takes a back seat to inauthentic harmony. Going along in order to keep the peace is a form of hiding the self. Erasing the self is an enormous sacrifice, one that can lead to anger and eventually to despair. Unconsciously, acts of self-forgetting feed anger, this type's primary emotional issue. Nines, for the most part, deny anger. It feels scary and uncontrollable, and Nines believe that anger severs connections. In Nines, anger may appear as stubbornness or passive-aggressive behavior. Befriending anger and exploring what drives it are entry points for accessing the full range of emotions and feeling alive. Tamping down the emotion of anger suppresses all other emotions.

"Will naming what I want disconnect me from you if what I want isn't what you want?" When Nines hear this inner narrative, it's a clue to engage both/and thinking. How might both agendas be honored? Both/and is a blind spot. Working with both/and thinking supports good decision making and clears a path for Nines to claim their priorities and desires and to set boundaries. Nines benefit from

planning into the next week to ensure that their priorities and wants get attention. This planning supports Nines in knowing and naming what they want. Otherwise, when the next week comes, they'll merge with others' agendas, once again forgetting themselves.

Nines' defense mechanism of narcotization brings a numbing effect that keeps the self-forgetting in play. The idea or act of self-remembering brings the fear of conflict. This fear leads to watchfulness and constant scanning for conflicts in order to "mediate" them before they occur. Deflecting, positive reframing, and finding common ground are methods used to keep the peace and avoid conflict. Others may not realize that Nines are mediating. When conflict between others does arise, Nines usually leave the room! For Nines, mediation consists of the subtle diverting or dissolving of tensions before a conflict arises. This type doesn't corner the market on the role of mediator, however. Every type has gifts for mediating, and with proper training we can all be skillful mediators. (For example, Fours' comfort with intense emotions and Fives' nonreactivity are great features in the role of mediator.)

Over the years, I've facilitated many type Nine groups. What has been most fascinating to me is the humor and aliveness in these groups. In gathering with other Nines, they all relax, knowing that no one will be confrontational. Their playful energy is a delight to witness. In these type groups, Nines come to realize that their impulse to scan for and mediate conflict pulls energy from them unnecessarily. More often than not, the conflict is nonexistent. In my work with Nines, I often hear them say "This will be hard . . ." when moving into an uncertain outcome. In reality, difficulties may not be forthcoming. Practices that serve to lessen this scanning tendency are worthy of engagement and can support Nines in learning to approach conversations with an expectation of kindness!

When faced with difficult conversations, Nines may want to *consider the positive aspects of conflict.* See the interaction as a problem-solving engagement rather than an argument that disconnects. When respect and curiosity are present, conflicts deepen relationships and birth creative options and possibilities.

The Core Fear and the Pivot

One of the most painful inner narratives that minimizes Nines is *"What if I show up, name my wants, and I'm ignored?"* An unconscious false belief that "I don't matter" is a core fear, and Nines develop a sensitivity to being dismissed. This fear of being neglected sets Nines up to neglect themselves, believing that "If I ignore me first, it will be less painful than if others ignore me." Recognizing this internal struggle can be a **compassionate entry point** in our relationships with Nines, as well as an entry point for their own self-compassion. In loving people who lead with this type structure, keep in mind the importance of including Nines, remembering them, and asking for their opinions. This grows the relationship and builds trust.

Sometimes, Nines believe they are being ignored when actually they do this to themselves and project their self-neglect onto others. When this belief surfaces, Nines might notice how they are minimizing themselves, making it difficult for others to see and hear them. Noticing themselves pulling back to listen or stepping aside when others are more energetic is an invitation for Nines to share themselves, state their wants, share their fears and concerns. Self-remembering is "the" courageous act for this type, risking showing up powerfully and clearly even when the outcome is unknown. Healing and wholeness begin when Nines shift into right action and name themselves as significant. Risking discomfort is an awakening in itself.

Nines: *Showing up allows others to know you and maybe, just maybe, love you more fully. Love awaits you when you risk visibility. Remember your significance!*

Companion Voices

As you read the stories from the companion writers, be open to finding a part of you in their shared experiences.

Our first contributor, **Claire,** has much to say about Nines' issues with anger and voicing their own agenda as she discovers herself anew in this glimpse into the life experiences of someone who leads with Nine.

I had been married maybe two or three years when my husband looked over at me one evening from across the living room as we turned on yet another show he'd convinced me to watch. We were in our early twenties, still relatively newlywed, and trying our best to understand one another. He made a gentle observation that, at the time, felt like a provocation. He said, "In these habits we've settled into in our down time, it seems like we mostly do things that I like to do, and you just sort of . . . come along for the ride. What is it that *you* like to do?"

I was immediately defensive. Sure, he was only asking what I liked to do for fun, but I heard the question resonating at a much deeper level, and it felt like an accusation. It wasn't that I was just struggling to identify a hobby I enjoyed; it felt like he was accusing me of being the kind of person who didn't know what she really wanted in life. (As it turned out, that was exactly the kind of person I was.) I agonized over it for weeks, though my agony wasn't exactly active; I wasn't out there trying new things to see if I liked them. I mostly just tormented myself with questions: What *did* I like to do? Why didn't I know? Was I a weak person for not having my own interests? Surely, though, I did have interests, wants, desires—so why couldn't I access them?

I hadn't yet been introduced to the Enneagram, but when I eventually gained the language to know that I lead with type Nine, I realized how that conversation with my husband had thrown into relief one of the major ways I would come to recognize my type in my day-to-day existence: the merging of my own desires, wants, and needs with the desires, wants, and needs of my spouse, colleagues, family—really anyone to walk within a 20-foot radius of me at any given moment. The work of spiritual awakening for me has been an ever-unfolding process of claiming my voice, my desires, and my own self. I have found that once I begin to do that work in one part of my life, the rest tends to follow. At least, that seems to be the case if the last two years are any indication.

Four years ago, I was approaching my 30th birthday as a white woman serving as a progressive Baptist pastor in the South (I know it sounds like an oxymoron, but believe me, we are real). That fall, I found myself tentatively voicing to my husband that despite my appearance as a happily married, straight woman, I might actually be a happily married, bisexual woman, and I wasn't sure what to do with that newfound revelation. I began journaling again with a renewed appreciation for the spiritual discipline of it, and found that in the daily nature of the task, I was gaining clarity and a sense of rootedness in myself. On the advice of my spiritual director, I began writing each day to record one thing that I wanted, gaining familiarity with the desires, large and small, that so often went unnoticed and unexplored in my life. Journaling has always been a fallback method of processing for me in difficult seasons, but journaling consciously with the awareness of the gifts and challenges of leading with Nine has been an incredible source of growth for me.

Then, we got an elliptical, and it changed my life—though not for the reasons you might expect. I stepped onto the elliptical hoping it would help me in all the ways one might anticipate physical exercise would help: getting in shape, getting those endorphins pumping, connecting with the psychological benefits of physical activity. What I didn't anticipate was how holistic the psychological benefits would be, and how much it would have to do with getting in touch with the anger I have such difficulty accessing inside myself. One day, I turned on a feminist documentary a friend had recommended as a way to make the exercise more bearable, and I noticed that the deeper the injustice on the screen was, the faster I ran. Next, it was music. Running to a catchy song with a steady beat is always a good way to pick up the pace, but turn on "Gaslighter" by the Chicks in the middle of the Trump administration and it was like I couldn't run fast enough to keep up with the anger propelling me forward. This was a new sensation for me.

I discovered that anger is a messenger telling us that a boundary is being crossed, or that something in our lives is out of line with the values we hold most deeply. For someone who struggles to access that anger, this realization turned a daily workout into a daily spiritual practice. On the elliptical, I'm already breathing heavily, already in touch with my body, so when I notice my body beginning to feel angry, there's nothing to stop me from running as fast and as hard as I need to run to let it out. What I've found is that the "letting it out" isn't the end of something, but rather a beginning. It's what puts me in touch with the message the anger carries, and I can take that consciousness with me back into my day, into the work that I do and my daily interactions. Given enough time, I also began to take it with me into bigger-picture decisions that would affect my career, my sense of vocation, and my own spiritual identity.

I learned that despite my outward appearance as a very mild-tempered, peacekeeping pastor, a lot of anger churned under the surface. And that anger had a lot to tell me about the answer to the questions that had been bugging me for years: What do I like to do? What is it that I want?

As it turned out, there were a whole lot of things I wanted, and most of them came back to a desire for honesty. I wanted to be more honest in the ways I showed up in the world. That meant I wanted to step down from my role as a pastor; I no longer wanted to be identified by my job title as a person who held a set of beliefs I hadn't held in quite some time. It meant I wanted to come out as bisexual, not for the sake of anyone else, but for myself, simply to embrace the gift of being myself wholeheartedly in this world, because my presence, my showing up, matters. It meant I wanted to get back in the classroom. I wanted to be in an environment where I could explore my intellectual curiosity about the ways that the white, heteronormative patriarchy that has shaped Christianity harms people in the pews and places where healing might be found. It's work that is giving me so much life—and it's work that only materialized when I gained access to the anger that was carrying such rich messages for me, buried in the depths of my spirit.

And believe it or not, my anger even found me a hobby! The scene in my living room most evenings may not look all that different at first glance. My husband and I still tend to sit across from one another watching a show or movie he's excited about, but I can now be found with an embroidery hoop in hand, working on my latest piece of snarky feminist cross-stitch. My latest project: a lovely mid-autumn birch tree just beginning to lose its leaves, with the caption, "My favorite season is the fall . . . of the patriarchy."

Can you sense the power of Claire claiming herself? Exercise plays a role in this, and she offers a good reminder of the importance of exercise for Nines. Physical activity that brings breath up into the chest has a way of clearing the mind's fogginess. Coming more fully into the body's sensations allows us all to remember ourselves, to notice who we are in the moment.

In the following companion contribution, **Theresa** describes how she engaged with the Nine's issue of significance as she becomes a beautiful bridge between cultures.

Most of my childhood through young adult life was spent internalizing voices around me telling me what I should and shouldn't be doing, what I was good and not good at, and where I should be headed with my life. There was little input from my own internal voice as I mainly sought to please others. I shied away from leadership roles and teamwork because I had trouble finding and sharing my own voice, especially when forced into the spotlight. I didn't feel confident in speaking my feelings because I didn't think they mattered enough to others. I thought if I did what others wanted of me, I was keeping them happy and therefore could create happiness in my own life. But I wasn't happy, and through long stretches of depression over the years, I often felt unheard, unseen, and undervalued.

In 2012, after relocating back to Richmond, Virginia, and completing a PhD in musicology at the University of Edinburgh, I found myself struggling. I had been in a structured higher education setting for years, which gave me a sense of purpose and placement in life. Now that I was free to make my own choices, I felt lost and without direction. I was easily led into thinking that the only satisfying vocation would be in an academic role all my degrees had led me toward. By 2016, I had worked a host of part-time jobs to make ends meet as I continued to search aimlessly for more sustainable academic employment. I had a nearly full-time load as an adjunct lecturer, commuting four days per week to a university 70 miles away, teaching yoga and Pilates classes at two local gyms, and teaching piano lessons at a children's music academy and privately at home, and I was about to take on yet another part-time role as a musician for a local church. I worked seven days a week, spending my evenings and weekends either teaching or prepping for the next day or next week. I was exhausted. But I had little energy to even think about what self-care meant, and instead continued to believe this overwork was expected in order to achieve some measured sense of "success." What I least suspected was that taking on the new role of organist/pianist at Grace Baptist Church in Richmond would not only shift my outlook on myself and my values, but also illuminate a new pathway to an unexpected calling.

Taking on a job in a church started out exactly as that: just another job to add to my growing list of employment. But this was no ordinary role for someone like me. And by "someone like me," I mean for someone who is a Muslim woman. It wasn't always easy being raised as a Muslim by an Iranian mother and English revert father in a predominantly white, Christian environment. Being white-presenting and without a *hijab*, I never wore my Muslim identity on my sleeve. As a result, it was often assumed that I was likely raised as a Christian—so much so that I was often privy to hurtful or ignorant comments targeted toward my faith and my heritage by people who had no idea I was "one of those." My type Nine tendencies only amplified my feelings of rejection and isolation as I focused on these discouraging voices. I felt alienated and misunderstood, and so I retreated and continued to keep my voice silent. At Grace Baptist Church, however, I was about to face a turning point in my life, an opening to new possibilities.

As a musician and an academic that leads with type Nine, I am no stranger to self-doubt. I often wondered if I was good enough—good enough to compete with others, good enough to be successful, good enough to sustain a livelihood, good enough to be accepted by others. I wasn't a confident performer, but I also felt conflicted when my music seemed to exist in a vacuum—between the freedom of being alone with my music and the solitary nature of practicing without a connection to others. Working at Grace Baptist has taught me that my musical gifts are not meant to stay in isolation; they are meant to be heard. I continue to be reminded that music does not have to be about perfection and aiming for an unattainable ideal. It is about human connection. So, I decided to come out of hiding myself and show up with my gifts. Every week, I play from my heart, making myself emotionally vulnerable through music. In response, I am met with overwhelming love and gratitude from both the ministerial staff and congregation at Grace, who are deeply moved by these musical experiences.

Buoyed by the appreciative support from those around me, I have learned to claim my own brand of "ministry" through music. In this process, I asked myself what I wanted and if I needed to continue in an unfulfilling academic role simply because it "looked good" on paper or because it was expected of me. In 2019, when the position of church administrator at Grace became vacant, I saw an opportunity to build upon my musical role and to take a healthy break from being stretched thin across multiple jobs and long commutes. I stopped listening to what I felt others expected of me and took a chance; I made a choice that was solely for me, for my mental and spiritual health. It was the best decision I could have made. My role continues to grow in ways I never expected, far beyond the titles of "church administrator" or "organist," to a vital part of a team that cultivates a genuine bond between members of the church and the community while inspiring deep connection between these worshipers and God. And as such, I feel greatly blessed and rewarded, more than ever before in my life.

In the past, I have found it easy to slip into the Nine cycle of feeling neglected and unappreciated after focusing on unconstructive external voices and trying to live up to the ideals of others. I have learned it is possible to shift the cycle to be one framed by positivity and support. As I learn to accept love and encouragement from others around me and tune out negativity, I see more clearly how my voice and my gifts matter, which inspires me to share other aspects of my identity. Now, I receive invitations to share freely about my Muslim faith practices and beliefs, and am met with genuine interest and curiosity. Even my academic research is more genuinely welcomed because of its ties to my unique cultural experiences. It is incredibly liberating to finally express my authentic self. The more open I am about myself, the more accepted and loved I feel, and so the cycle of support goes. *It seems that authenticity leads to loving connections!*

Responding to the quote by Miles Davis, "Man, sometimes it takes a long time to sound like yourself," musician and community activist Greg Jarrell writes, "Sounding like yourself is not the sort of work done by yourself. . . . It takes a whole community of friends and companions to help you learn who you are and what you have to say."[1] I am 38 at the time of writing this, and I can't find a better way to sum up how I have found my voice through my work. I have found my community in Grace Baptist Church, a place where love abounds and where welcome and celebration (not just acceptance) reign. Every person is encouraged to come as they are and to be true to themselves in the eyes of God, and that is something worthy of celebrating. This place has become my second home. The congregation has *welcomed* a young Muslim woman to participate in worship, contribute to its planning and church leadership. Without question, they trust me.

By witnessing how community comes together in such loving and accepting ways, I realize that I am not an island, and I do not have to nor am I expected to do everything alone. As a result, I now take better care of myself mentally, taking the time to refuel in order to continue to build upon my newfound ministry. My gifts now shine in a different light than they ever have in the past. I use music as a vehicle to unite people in their grief and sorrow, joy and hope, and create a deeper worship experience. Beyond that, my work and my voice now signify bridge building between faiths and cultures, creating greater awareness of interfaith practices, of the commonalities between faiths, and a better understanding of multicultural experiences.

This shift from believing "I don't matter" to making a significant impact is inspirational. Theresa demonstrates the strength of Nines and the impact they have on others when they risk showing up fully in themselves.

Alchemy: From Type to Essence

Holy Love as Enlightened Spiritual Perspective

The shift from self-forgetting to self-remembering is *right action* that allows Nines to see the significance of their lives and to risk discomfort and conflict. Seeing through the sacred lens of Holy Love, their love for others begins with self-love. When Nines know that they, too, are loved unconditionally, they demonstrate an engaged receptivity that feels alive. For all of us, *claiming* requires waking up to ourselves, to what is most important in our lives. Paradoxically, although it would seem that claiming takes energy, Nines report that when they show up, they find they have *more* energy. Claiming is a powerful energetic force. "I am here!" This is Nines' gift to our world.

Arriving in Holy Love, Nines know their significance, their lovability. From this knowing, they become our teachers in giving and receiving love unconditionally. This loving presence is powerful. This love invites us all to risk being seen, risk being loved, in order to live with aliveness.

Claiming is a deep honoring of who we are, and it takes us to the deep wells of inner resources and our Essence. "If I show up, I'll be loved." How would our behavior change if we truly believed this?

PRACTICES Bringing Awareness to Nines' Core Issues

Focused Inquiry

+ *What tells you that you are hiding behind harmony? What allows you to risk visibility?*
+ *When has the need to keep the peace been a barrier to your loving fully?*
+ *How might your anger be your gateway to love?*

Our practices are ways of saying "yes" to our journey to our Essence.

Engagement to Counter the Type's Patterns

+ Slowly and deliberately, begin deleting from your vocabulary the word "whatever" and the phrase "it doesn't matter to me." If, in the moment, you don't know what you want, then ask for time to think.
+ Using the alphabet, name something specific that you want that begins with each letter. For example, using

the letter "a," what do you want? Art supplies? A certain kind of apple? Work with four letters each week. This is a simple, effective exercise for waking up Nines to their wants.

- Notice when you are procrastinating. Break down the task into small chunks, creating deadlines for each. Smaller portions can be easier to tackle. Procrastination feels heavy, and getting things done lightens the mood. To this end, *at the end of your day, do one more thing.* Whether it's sending an email, making a phone call, or organizing a corner of your space, take 15 minutes and do one more thing before you end your day. This advice comes from a type Nine group!
- When you feel excitement, stay with it. Allow it to rise. Experience it as life force.
- Journal at the end of the day about how you mattered to yourself and to others. Notice how it feels to matter and to be seen.
- When you become angry about being ignored, discern if your anger is with yourself or another. How would you redo this situation?
- Each week, spend an hour planning the next week. Include your priorities and wants in your planning.

Often, Nines think and respond in generalities. For instance, tasked with setting a realistic intention for self-care for a week, I've heard Nines say, "I'll be kind to myself." This isn't specific enough. Ask yourself, *"What does self-kindness look like? When will I engage in this behavior?"* Inquiring into the "what," "when," and "how" of an intention can lead to specificity. **Growth for Nines hinges on structures and specifics.**

> ## BEYOND YOUR TYPE
>
> *Your great love within (that includes yourself) matters and makes a significant impact.*

Sabbath-Keeping

Sabbath, in the traditional Jewish understanding, directs our focus to awe and provides space for us to cultivate delight in creation and our lives. Sabbath invites us to wake up to ourselves and our world.

This day is structured to support Nines' waking up to themselves and clearing away the inessentials that distract. Structure is key and offers opportunities for Nines to become more conscious of how inertia influences their lives. (When in motion, you can't stop. When stopped, it's difficult to begin.) Sabbath day involves, first and foremost, moving the body. Whether through a brisk walk, a run in the neighborhood, or an exercise routine, *vigorously* engage your body. (Walking the dog does not count.) Set aside a specific time for this. Avoid activities that allow you to numb out, like watching TV, internet activity, or talking on the phone.

Name one thing that would delight you today, and initiate making that happen *now*! Invite another to join you, but make all of the decisions regarding the what, when, where, and how yourself.

Take time during this Sabbath day to review the next week's schedule. What are your priorities? Identify tasks, meetings, and activities that are unnecessary and eliminate them from your week. This means making time to say "no." Don't allow other activities to lengthen and slide into the time you've freed up. Instead, choose a personal priority that you want to fulfill and create a plan for making that happen, naming a specific time and coming up with a strategy. Time saved from the unnecessary busyness makes time for your own priorities in your own life.

A Type Nine Prayer

Create in me a refuge for remembering myself, a safe place where I can go deep and explore the full range of who I am. Ground of Being, dissolve my fears of anger so that I may allow it to guide me in knowing what matters to me and what the matter is. Empty me now of my resistance to my inner journey, my resistance to waking up to my life. Remind me of my own lovability, so that in loving myself, I may genuinely love others, and in this loving show up in the peaceful times and in the difficult times. I no longer want to deprive myself of my joy. Spirit, be my foundation as I honor my life and my relationships by offering my aliveness and my fullness.

CHAPTER 5

The Power of Opening: Type Eight

When people first learn about the Enneagram, I've noticed an adherence to a rigid stereotype of type Eight. If someone is angry or abusive, they must be an Eight, right? Absolutely not! "Who do you have in mind when you say this?" I usually ask. Often, I've heard other types state, "I went to my Eight and got angry." Nines will commonly refer to their Eight wing when they access their own anger. As we continue to explore the Enneagram and add depth to our understanding of the nine types, these initial caricatures dissolve. We project less and claim more of who we are, including our anger. As you read this chapter, invite the type Eight within you to listen in.

TYPE EIGHT AT A GLANCE

Strengths: Bold, confident, generous, energetic
Ego Ideal: I am strong.
Focus of Attention: What is out of control
Motivation: To protect self and others from vulnerability
Worldview: The world is a jungle that destroys the weak.
Fixation: Blame
Vice: Lust
Holy Idea: Holy Truth
Virtue: Innocence (unguarded and open)

Brief Overview

Eights are fiercely caring people. They are loyal and generous to those they love. With easy access to their life force, energy rises quickly and without effort. This energy can be intense, yet when it is grounded, Eights demonstrate a tender strength. If you've witnessed an Eight with a small child or an animal, you have seen this tenderness emerge. When others experience hard times, Eights are there, bringing their practical selves, support, and grounded presence.

Like Ones and Nines, Eights are self-forgetting. This shows up in physical fatigue or being unaware of emotional fragility. The ego ideal of "I am strong" suggests to Eights that "I can take it," so they maintain their forward motion, further forgetting themselves. My friend Lee, who leads with Eight, likes to say "I'm in fifth gear or face down." Eights expend lots of energy during the day and generally are passionately in or not engaged at all. Learning to manage energy is common growth work for Eights. Moderation is an unfamiliar concept that raises the questions: *When do you use more energy than is needed? What tells you this?*

Lust is the vice or passion for this type, and it brings a gusto to living. Lust is an impulsive drive to have a need satisfied now, with the emphasis on *now!* This understanding of lust may or may not pertain to sex. The need for certainty, a quick decision, and immediate action are indicators that lust is in the driver's seat. When lust is in control, Eights are blind to options and focused solely on the sought-after goal. Leading with Eight, I've noticed that it's best not to get between me and a Dairy Queen Blizzard on a hot summer's day! I want it now. A "later" approach rarely shows up on the radar. Lust has both a certainty and an urgency to it. Neither arises from presence, but from a grasping to have a desire quickly satisfied. Eights may benefit from practicing later.

Eights are the most protected and armored type on the Enneagram Map, avoiding vulnerability for fear of being treated unjustly. Most Eights understand that a tender heart resides in them. However, Eights tend to forget that their tender heart is also strong. Thus, they overprotect. Fast action feels safe and is a form of protecting and controlling. Believing in the worldview that those in power treat the fragile unfairly, taking control before another does seems logical to Eights. To feel safe, Eights act to direct the outcome. Uncertainty produces anxiety and is not an option. Understanding that fear drives the desire to direct and take control is a **compassionate entry point** when relating to Eights. Gentle, honest questions in these times can be helpful in expanding an Eight's awareness. If you lead with type Eight, notice the anxiety driving your impulse to control and direct. In this moment, wait one minute before speaking or acting and breathe through the anxiety.

A key discernment for this type is to understand when directing is needed and when waiting is the appropriate response. When directing is reactive and thoughtless, it springs from fear and is a barrier to the heart. To soften the impulse to direct, Eights might explore who and what situations draw out the controlling response. *With whom am I directive? In what kinds of situations does the impulse to control rise quickly? What would happen if I didn't direct? When have I benefited by others directing the outcome? When have I benefited from waiting?*

The Striving and the Avoidance

Striving for Eights lies in the need or desire to make an impact. This can appear as stating opinions, having the first or the final word in a conversation, helping another, or righting a wrong. Making an impact masks feelings of vulnerability. While making things happen is one of the gifts of this type, Eights may be unaware that this constant impacting can be wearing on others as well as tiring to themselves. Their energetic intensity can be too much; it's like cooking on high all the time. The ego ideal of "I am strong" motivates Eights' striving to make an impact and give the appearance of strength. When in the grip of that inner narrative, it may be useful to consider: *How patient is my strength? How flexible am I right now?* If strength isn't patient and flexible, options fade, and strength becomes a show of force rather than an internal support.

The need to control and to make an impact is in the background of the "no" that Eights can express when someone offers an idea or solution. An inner anxiety arises quickly and causes pushback when Eights haven't had time to think through an issue that arises in the moment. Often, this "no" isn't their last word. With a bit of time, Eights may reevaluate their support for the other's idea or solution.

The defense mechanism for Eights is denial, which creates a blindness to their own lack of strength or competitive edge. It works to keep vulnerability in the background. Eights cannot see what's before them when in denial's grip. Nothing seems impossible. Often the path of ease isn't in view. An example of denial that I witnessed years ago was a type Eight politician who ran for a US Senate seat against a strong incumbent. Everyone except this individual was aware of the high likelihood that the incumbent would be reelected. Denial maintained its blinders until the end, when the seat was held by the incumbent—a surprising outcome to the Eight.

The Core Fear and the Pivot

Whether conscious or not, Eights' fear of being powerless (and unjustly controlled) is a driver behind the need to overprotect their hearts. Usually, when Eights' energy amps up to dominate or move into excess, they are scared. As one Eight said, "When I am too much, I am often hiding the inner feeling of being too small (vulnerable)." For all of us, vulnerability is scary. Eights mistakenly equate this with being weak, a posture in opposition to their ego ideal and therefore to be avoided at all costs. Puffing oneself up to appear confident or certain is a common Eight strategy. When I notice myself leaning forward, my body contracting and my tone intense, I realize that these are cues that my confidence is sinking. This is my invitation to sit back, become more curious, and listen for possibilities. Easier said than done!

Eights often put their "truth" or opinion out there, so when they can't influence others or an outcome, they fear being irrelevant (powerless). This may manifest as impatience, irritability, or anger. In these moments, others can support Eights by repeating their words back to them so they feel heard and relevant. This type creates dualities quickly, one being a mental framework of "with me" or "against me." Those of us leading with Eight can support ourselves by noticing this inner narrative in the moment and staying engaged in the conversation, seeking to understand rather than listening for agreement or disagreement. When relating to Eights, if you notice this "against stance," use it as a **compassionate entry point** and demonstrate to the Eight, through body language and words, your companionship, your *withness*.

Dualistic thinking (*with or against*) is breeding ground for the Eight's fixation of blame. Blaming the other serves to give Eights a hit of strength, a feeling of being powerful. Blame thickens the armor. Naming a wrong or an injustice is seductive, as it invites Eights' opinions (small truths) and impactful action. If Eights can resist this seduction and move into curiosity, they can realize that *blame is a lame response* to a situation that is more complex than it appears. *Pivoting to curiosity* in these moments allows Eights to move toward the virtue of innocence. Innocence is an open, unguarded posture. No opinion, no certainty exists. Opening to the wisdom and goodness of others, Eights soften. A tender heart emerges and mercy abounds.

When asked about her leadership style in the *New York Times*, Lynn Jurich, the CEO of Sunrun Solar, replied, "All people and all circumstances are my allies."[1] If we truly believed in this *withness*, how would our behavior change?

Eights: *Vulnerability and a willingness to be touched offer a new kind of power and beauty that can emerge in the practice of waiting.*

Companion Voices

As you read the stories from the companion writers, be open to finding a part of you in their shared experiences.

If you have been reading this book in order, you have read the companion voices of the Nines. The following type Eight voices offer a different style and approach. Both speak to a mother's love, to the mama bear role in relating to daughters. In this first contribution, **Satoya,** through use of a narrative format, shares her life's journey and teaches us about her strength, denial, and tenderness. Please note, this piece includes content related to violence and child abuse.

I am a first-generation Jamaican American. This identity is interesting to reconcile, as my distinctiveness causes me to fall between the "cracks" of Jamaican American. My reality is that I am neither Jamaican nor American enough to be considered a whole person by others. Born into a Caribbean community in New York, I ate oxtail with rice and peas, manish wata, ackee, and saltfish. I also consumed quarter waters, bacon-egg-n-cheese (because in New York, this is basically one word), and five-cent candies in a brown paper bag from Papi at the corner store.

My parents owned a laundromat in a shopping plaza. They also drove a gypsy van that raced the city bus to pick up passengers, offering a cheaper fare than the bus. We appeared to be a hard-working, immigrant, church-going family, but in reality, we were barely surviving.

The house I was raised in was violent and chaotic. As the youngest and only girl of four, I didn't have the privilege of being donned with the "spoiled" mantle that generally seems to fall upon the youngest child. I had strict Jamaican parents and needed to be strong and clever since the boys were all older and bigger than me. As a child, if I felt bullied by my brothers, I would patiently wait until the opportune time to pounce and repay any previous unkindnesses.

Reflecting on my formative years into adulthood, I can easily identify the Eight's defense mechanism of denial. Denial operated to limit my ability to allow myself to be or recognize the ways I am impacted by anything or anyone outside of myself.

I am not weak. I am strong. I am not affected. I can protect myself.

I was treated harshly as a child and beaten regularly. The elapsed time and severity of the beatings seemed to correlate with the level of frustration and anger I seemingly caused. The more regular beatings involved getting hit with a leather belt across extended arms. At first, I would cry. As tears rolled down my face, I would hear, *"Yuh wan mi gi yuh sumting fi cry bout?"*

Eventually, I stopped crying. I would feel the bitter sting of the belt across my arms and swallow the pain to rob them of any satisfaction of seeing my suffering. The more escalated beatings involved fists, fan belts, and anything else in arm's reach. On one occasion, I assumed that my father grew tired of the typical disciplinary tools because he creatively twisted a wire and wrapped tape around one end until it resembled a mace. Cornered in a small bathroom in the laundromat, I could not escape the severity of his beating.

I am not weak. I am strong. I am not affected. I can protect myself.

A few days after my 18th birthday, I moved out of my parents' house carrying only a book bag after being threatened for the last time. I always knew I would leave as soon as I could, and this was the moment. I was with my boyfriend and a few friends when my phone rang. I answered.

"Hello?"

"Where yuh deh?" my mother shouted at the other end of the phone. I could hear my father incoherently rambling in the background. My mother yelled that one of my brothers was coming to pick me up. I knew in my body that it was time. About 15 minutes later, my phone rang again.

"Sis, I'm outside."

"I'm not coming . . ."

"You sure?" he said with surprise.

"Yes," with resolve.

We hung up, and I sat with my boyfriend and friends, wide-eyed and free-ish. After taking a moment to revel in the power and trepidation I felt, I said, "We gotta go." My father didn't take kindly to perceived disrespect, so we needed to leave. I figured he would probably drive around the city looking for me and lurking in the places he thought I'd go. I quickly gathered up my few belongings, then my friends and I went for a drive, away from my familiar places.

I am not weak. I am strong. I am not affected. I can protect myself.

For a few years, I was part of a band that toured the Northeast and Midwest. Once, during the tour, my father called shortly after 10 p.m. I stayed on the phone with him until the sun came up because he was spewing all manner of evils about harming my mother and picturing himself in an orange jumpsuit. Since I didn't know where my mother was, I kept him on the phone for hours in hopes of distracting him from harming her.

Shortly after returning from the tour, I moved my mother out of the house while she was at work. Leading with type Eight, I can feel a sense of certainty, which often arises from fear. I felt certain that she needed to move. I would make it happen. While I did this without her consent, I believed I was helping her. I still kinda think so.

After bagging up her belongings and putting them in my car, I called my mother. *"Come to my house. You now live with me."* I was the protective daughter keeping her safe.

I am not weak. I am strong. I am not affected. I can protect myself.

I got married shortly before my 21st birthday. Weeks later, my mother filed for divorce. My father still lived in their marital home. One day, my mom needed to check the mail. The street was vacant of streetlights and the house was dark. My mother drove the car as I sat in the passenger's seat. She pulled up slowly to the house and stopped. I lowered my window and quickly grabbed the mail. My mom took the mail and said, *"Go and look in the garage to see if his car is there."* My eyes widened, and I looked through the window at the dark garage. My mind raced and my heart sank. I put my hand on the door to open it, but I couldn't. We sat quietly in the car for a few moments. Breaking the silence, my mom asked, *"Yuh scared?"*

I am not weak. I am strong. I am not affected. I can protect myself.

I didn't answer. In this moment, I felt a deep rage in me. How dare she ask me this? The truth was, I was angry that she asked me to admit that I was afraid. Admitting my fear went against everything I had worked so hard to build—a wall so high and wide I believed it was impenetrable.

I felt weak and vulnerable. I didn't feel strong. I was affected. I could not protect myself.

This was a pivotal moment when my vulnerability emerged and all of my resolve came crashing down. Throughout my life, my type Eight structure supported me in taking care of myself. My life circumstances taught me that I needed to be strong. In order to support this strength, I learned to deny any vulnerability or perception of weakness in myself.

The Eight's idealized self, "I am strong," kept me alive and safe. After years of traumatic experiences, I thought I was strong and could handle anything. For a while, I did. But it also kept me from being open and receptive to some of my deeper desires of joy and ease. In maintaining my strength, I had limited my ability to fully connect with others. If I desired to engage the more tender parts of myself—my creativity, inner joy, my desire to be loved in the palpable ways I loved others—I had to allow vulnerability a space in my life.

Therapy played a significant role in my healing process. Years later, in learning the Enneagram, I became aware of the type Eight defense patterns within me. The Enneagram gave me language and a path toward awareness, understanding, and healing. Utilizing the Enneagram in my therapeutic process helped accelerate my awareness and growth.

Deeper realizations came after I gave birth to my daughter. When I looked into her eyes, I saw her vulnerability and innocence and felt her full reliance on me. I sensed her delight in me and her wonderment of the world around her. Experiencing this, I thought of my responsibility to protect her in every way. At that moment, I hadn't yet realized that the vulnerability and innocence I was seeing in her eyes reflected my own lost innocence and wonder. I felt my rage.

Raising my daughter has made a profound difference in my life. She has been the biggest catalyst of change in my life. When she's hurt or sad, I comfort her. When she's crying, I hold her. She invites me to play, dance, be silly, and make mistakes. She teaches me to be curious and to come to things with fresh eyes and an open heart. Over time, my softness and vulnerability became more prominent.

By comforting and holding her, I learned to comfort and hold myself. By engaging her curiosity, I began to engage my curiosity. Through seeing her innocence and wonder, I began to see and experience my own. These new feelings and experiences didn't mean that I wasn't strong anymore. They meant that my ability to be open and affected by people and things outside of me was included in my strength.

Over time, my self-compassion has grown, and I'm learning to pause to create space between myself and my reactions. The space between myself and my Eight armor makes room for all of the connectedness I was missing. I feared losing my idealized self—I am strong and powerful—which kept me safe and alive in my earlier years. Now I know that vulnerability is not an absence of strength, but a deep call to compassionate care, connection, and abiding love.

Satoya reminds us of the power in pausing to create internal spaciousness. This isn't easy for one who experiences child abuse. Pausing, then opening, is truly courageous for Satoya. Her daughter reminds Satoya of the power of love and expands her understanding of strength. Children hold up a mirror that can be a vehicle for deepening inner awareness and engaging in transformative work.

As I considered contributors for this publication, I decided to invite a mother/daughter pair who lead with the same Enneagram type to share some of their story together. **Lee** and her daughter **Laurel**, in a conversation with each other, teach us about the dynamic between an Eight mother and an Eight daughter. The intensity, passion, and love are palpable in their writing.

Lee (mother) to Laurel (daughter):

You were precocious in your language, and from your first words there was a clarity of intention and a standing of your ground that was striking. When you were a little over a year old, I remember listening to you putting yourself to sleep by practicing saying "no" in a range of inflections—loud, soft, playful, forceful, delighted. "No, no, no, no." You developed more words, but the certainty of that litany never changed. My mother told me some version of the same story about myself as a child. I didn't know the Enneagram at the time, but it is clear that the zest and the force of our Eightness is something we both manifested early on.

The dance of our wills and intensities has been variously triggering, elucidating, and joyous. From your first breath, I have loved you fiercely and wanted above all to give you what you needed to live your own life fully. In a strange circle, the intensity of that love has motivated me to take a deeper look at my own intensity. I have worked, with varying success, to temper my reflex to take charge and to protect based on my view of the world, knowing that given free rein, those aspects of myself could be stifling to the emergence of who my children are.

In thinking about the dialogue for this contribution, I excavated one of my journals from decades ago. A recent reading of journal entries reminded me of the process of working to moderate myself in the face of your force with the hope of providing you needed structure without excessive constriction.

"Laurel tells me that I have a way of 'being rude' and correcting her that she hates. This always comes at a time when she has pushed a limit or ignored a request about ten times, so I feel righteously entitled to lay it down starkly. But I need to go back and talk to her, to try and understand what she is trying to tell me about what I do, so that I can set the limits that need setting without doing so in a way that is unnecessarily harsh. I'll try again tomorrow."

On a better day, I wrote, "I am grateful for Laurel's will. For the fierceness of her sense of herself. Let me learn to experience that not as a barrier to be overcome but a powerful force which can guide and protect her as she learns to harness it."

I am grateful for the impetus that motherhood gave me to look inward, to look square in the face at my potential for becoming so enamored of my own certainty and force that in my forward motion I might mow over those I love with the best of intentions.

We continued that dance through your early years and mid-adolescence. You regularly told me how annoying I was, and without belaboring the details, there was a lot of mutual stepping on toes throughout. By the time you left for college, we were on more solid ground.

Laurel to Lee:

As a kid, I was a great sleeper. It came easily, steadily, nightly. I remember a night—I must have been about 15—when sleep escaped me. You and I were beginning to emerge from the testy period of my early adolescence. When I couldn't sleep, I called you and you came to my bed. You had me picture a boat sailing in my belly. I was charmed by what I found when I drew my attention downward, inward. It was vast, and it had a strong voice. That night I slept.

My body talks to me all the time, in that way that precedes language. From you, I learned to look inward and to listen to what arises. When I summon this memory, I recall my delight at what I found when I moved my attention from my head to my body. Equally delightful was surrender to guidance, acceptance of support, putting somebody else at the wheel. From that night, I began to carry a sensory memory of the relief and release of letting go of tight control, both of releasing my mind to my body and my vulnerability to you. A part of that memory is the felt sense of the gentleness with which you partnered with me. Had you been too directive, too much an authority, too much a psychologist, I would have never surrendered the wheel. Something about the softness allowed me to release without clenching.

When I think of you, it is often of your directness, your looking me dead in the eye and calling it as it is. But in the moments of my vulnerability, you come with a gentleness and a steady assurance that is grounding, that helps me find my way back to myself. You are not a subtle person, but I have required subtle mothering. Your strength and your softness have been equal teachers guiding me to value both in myself.

Lee to Laurel:

For me, our relationship shifted significantly and moved to more equal footing when your dad and I separated. The marriage and family had been foundational for me, deeply trusted and my safe space. When it imploded, I was devastated. I knew you were blindsided, and I felt urgency to provide protection and solace. We were both a wreck. Although you were not living at home at the time, I remember a period of weeks after the separation when you were at home with me more than you were away. As raw as that time was, I also remember it with tenderness. We spent a lot of time in our pajamas. We binge-watched *Arrested Development*. We drank tea. We drank wine. We slept in the same bed. We cried. We keened. We also laughed. The boundaries between who was taking care of whom felt fluid. I remember a certainty that as awful as this felt, neither of us doubted that we would both emerge upright and moving forward. There was a lack of self-consciousness in the pain and in the need for giving and receiving of care. I didn't have the words for it then, but now I would say that it was during that hard time when I understood that we were equals in our capacities for strength and vulnerability. In that shared space was profound safety.

Laurel to Lee:

I moved through my childhood and adolescence knowing that our family was rock solid. The news that you and dad were separating was abrupt, absolutely unanticipated, and shattering. The four of us, my sister and I, you and Dad, sat in the family room. He said the words, the air rushed out of me, and I felt a simultaneous constriction and eruption from my throat. Then your face contorted and you began to wail. I remember thinking that you looked and sounded like an animal.

In the weeks that followed, I needed to be near you. I was blindsided by this dissolution of our family as I had known it, and I wanted to return to the nest—to feel the sensory safety of home, and to be mothered. What happened instead, I think, was that we spent a period of weeks being animals together. We ate what was needed to sustain us, and no more—we weren't hungry. One or both of us would burst into sobs with little warning. We stayed in close physical proximity, stepping away from one another, but then quickly returning and reassuring with touch. We laughed a lot—hard, body-rocking laughs that punctuated tears—because we were devastated, but we were still funny as hell. The membrane between us thinned, and I remember emerging from those weeks feeling upright and accompanied. I felt it again when dad died. Again, I returned to the nest you provide; again, I felt devastated and firmly rooted in equal measure. The rawness of our vulnerabilities and losses has left me surer of my own strength, and of yours.

Between us:

We are 35 years into this shared journey, and it now feels like a meeting of equals. We come together in all our bigness. We gently hold one another's smallnesses. We trust one another to set good limits. When one oversteps, we trust the other to name it. We trust one another's mastery of self. We trust our intentions with one another. We trust one another's honesty and goodness of heart. It is dramatically safe. We love the ease with which we live in our bodies. We laugh hard, dance, and move without restraint. We savor food, color, and sound. We are blunt, we are tender, we are forceful, we are vulnerable. It is a rich and protected space we have mutually created, and it is one of the greatest gifts of our lives.

As a body type, Eights sense energy in another and can match it. Leading with Eight, both Laurel and Lee matched the other's energy, whether sadness, delight, bluntness, or any number of primal instincts showed up. This mirror supported an intimate connection between them. Life force flows easily with Eights—"we dance, we move without restraint." As adults, their relationship is more mutual, arising from the inner awareness each has cultivated.

Alchemy: From Type to Essence

Holy Truth as Enlightened Spiritual Perspective

Holy Truth is the truth of oneness, of unity. The world is nondual. There is no one to blame and nothing to challenge in a framework of Oneness. This understanding that we are not separate selves, but a part of the Oneness, dissolves walls of armor. Innocence, Eight's virtue, then arises as an unguarded, open posture. Opinions cease. Curiosity leads. When Eights relax into this enlightened spiritual perspective, they become the teachers of nonduality. The heart is more accessible and trust comes more easily with the understanding of unity. Mercy, gentle strength, and an openhearted living arise in this Oneness.

Opening to themselves and others comes naturally when Eights trust themselves. The power in an open posture lies in the space it creates for more wisdom and creativity to emerge. We need only to awaken to possibility. In opening, Eights can be affected by others, can be touched by unexpected kindness. This opening supports an Eight in knowing that the heart is not only tender, but strong. In the opening, Eights recognize that they are carried. Opening is a gateway to real strength, the strength that arises from flexibility, patience, and vulnerability.

PRACTICES Bringing Awareness to Eights' Core Issues

Focused Inquiry

- *Who are those people in your life who have your back and, in their own way, protect and abide with you?*
- *What do you sacrifice in your life by keeping vulnerability at a distance?*
- *When has the need to protect been a barrier to your loving fully?*
- *How do you discern between weakness and vulnerability?*
- *How does gentle strength feel in your body? What image comes to mind when you think of gentle strength?*

Our practices are ways of saying "yes" to our journey to our Essence.

Engagement to Counter the Type's Patterns

+ Practice engaging others with questions rather than declarations and opinions.
+ In conversations, look for connections and common ground rather than points of disagreement or ways to challenge.
+ In conversations, tone matters. As often as you can, soften your tone.
+ Check in with yourself three times each day, noticing your fatigue level and any emotions that are just beneath the surface.
+ At the end of each day, ask yourself, *"How was my heart touched today?"*
+ Notice when you reach out to others who may be sad or hurting, and check within to see if your tender self needs some attention.
+ Notice the moment when you're about to engage in a task, and consider doing this later.

Eights lose themselves and their gentle, playful spirit to a list of tasks. Lust arises to "get 'er done." A day without tasks makes space to connect with the heart and for kindness to self and others to emerge.

BEYOND YOUR TYPE

In claiming the power of a strong and tender heart, you offer a magnanimous spirit woven into generosity.

Sabbath-Keeping

Sabbath, in the traditional Jewish understanding, directs our focus to awe and provides space for us to cultivate delight in creation and our lives. Sabbath invites us to wake up to ourselves and our world.

This day's rhythm is designed to soften the Eight's intensity and dissolve the demands of lust. Lust fills time, rushes you toward the next task, project, person to assist, or whatever is desired *now*. Today is a day of no initiation and no agenda. Having no deadlines or agendas takes away the "bait" for lust. There is nothing to make happen today. Simply be receptive to what shows up. Allow others to do for you and gracefully receive. This is a small step in allowing another to care for you, to protect you. This does not indicate weakness. Be willing to experience your own fragility as you allow the support of others to surface, knowing this allowing isn't weakness but a mutual dance of protecting and loving. We all need and desire this mutuality. Receptivity isn't weakness. It is a grounding of self, not a crumbling.

The unconscious fear of inner deadness has Eights amping up life, going for the gusto each moment, and the body can take a beating as Eights tend to be unaware of the body's fatigue. As the 13th-century poet Jalal al-Din Rumi wrote, "You are burning up your soul to keep the body delighted."[2] Sabbath for Eights must include rest for the body. Cook if you like, or read, but most of all, rest your body. Be gentle with your body and tender with your heart.

A Type Eight Prayer

Ground of Being, make your presence known to me as I wade into the waters of uncertainty, for I do not trust easily. Empty me of my need to assert myself and my need to blame others when things don't go as I wish. Soften the walls surrounding my heart, the rigid boundaries, my strong opinions. Embrace me in my waiting, so that I may know the richness in stillness and open my heart to the affection of others. May I be present in each moment without judgment and without fear, knowing that my heart is strong. Ground me in a gentle and loving presence that I may be gentle and loving with myself and others. Remind me each day that we are all one and that in our unity we find hope, and in vulnerability we discover loving support.

CHAPTER 6

The Power of Accepting: Type One

Type One is one of the three Enneagram types that seem to get the most bad press (along with Four and Eight). I would be wealthy if I had a quarter for every time I've heard a workshop participant say something like "I went to my One and became judging and critical," or "My father was so critical, he had to be a One." Truth be told, we all are judging and critical. We judge the Ones for judging! When we do our own inner work, we see entry points for compassion when we witness Ones in a judging frame of mind. Remember, "as above, so below." The degree to which we criticize others correlates to the degree we critique ourselves. As you read this chapter, invite the type One within you to come forward.

TYPE ONE AT A GLANCE

Strengths: Reliable, detail-oriented, fair-minded, diplomatic

Ego Ideal: I am responsible and good.

Focus of Attention: Disorder, error

Motivation: To improve

Worldview: The world is chaotic and needs improving.

Fixation: Judging

Vice: Anger

Holy Idea: Holy Perfection

Virtue: Serenity

Brief Overview

Those who lead with type One have offered me the most nonjudgmental presence when I've strayed from myself, making one misstep after another. They were my steady friends, awaiting my return to myself. A nonjudging, steady presence is one of their great gifts to the world. They are not fair-weather friends. They have staying power. As a fair-minded type, Ones can be diplomatic and supportive, and patient with those who are devoted to learning and growing.

Ones are thoughtful in speech, decisions, and actions. They are responsible and deliberate, not impulsive. A strong drive to "be a good person and do right" creates high internal standards that give rise to rules and expectations, named or unnamed. And, as my mentor Dr. Daniels would often say, expectations create unrealized resentments. Resentment, or anger, is the vice of this type, often showing up as impatience or frustration. Usually, Ones judge anger as wrong and suppress it; thus, tight neck and shoulder muscles and a tense jaw are common ailments. Suppressed anger feels permanent, and Ones report a sense within themselves of a simmering frustration or low-grade anger. Suppression of one's emotion invites suppression of other emotions along with it. Joy, sadness, tenderness, delight, and other feelings are tamped down as righteous indignation leads the charge.

Strict adherence to moral convictions, drivenness, and reforming are channels for anger. A strong inner critic "stands against" reality and directs Ones toward mental categories of right and wrong, good and bad, fair and unfair, appropriate and inappropriate. The fixation of judging is connected to the vice of anger. When one is present, the other is as well. The inner critic can focus outward, inward, or both ways. However, when it is directed outward to judge others, this judgment is a projection. When the inner critic is directed inward, it may feel so devastating to the One that, to ease their inner turmoil, they turn it outward. One of the key projections for Ones is the belief that others are judging them. More often than not, this is a false conviction. For all of us, it's important to remember that judgment of another is, usually, a judgment of ourselves.

Ones are self-forgetting. Their responsibilities come first. Anger can be a clue that Ones may have substituted being responsible for experiencing pleasure. In his 30-plus years in psychiatric practice, Dr. Daniels observed this often in patients leading with type One. So, he drove this point home each time he led a type One panel. When Ones become aware of their self-deprivation, or self-forgetting, a good practice is to consider the "wants" that have been replaced by "shoulds," then attend to those desires. Naming your wants and making them a reality, even before your responsibilities are completed, is the right thing to do! Many Ones report that when on vacation and leaving responsibilities behind, they can throw caution to the wind and enjoy the moment, becoming excellent playmates.

Ones have an internal belief that "I am the responsible adult"—hence their tendency to postpone pleasure until their world is right again. At times, Ones believe that play equals irresponsibility. Those of us who love Ones know that a **compassionate entry point** is inviting them into spaces of relaxation, play, or a midday break from work. When Ones shift their focus from duty to delight, they see that fun can stimulate their creative juices and benefit their work. Joy awaits.

The Striving and the Avoidance

Ones' ego structure sets them up to be good, achieve, and get things right. Their focus of attention narrows their view to all that is in disarray or wrong. With this limited view of reality, Ones strive to fix, improve, and make the world right in order to avoid making mistakes or being inappropriate. This striving is a wrong turn. It pushes aside emotions and reduces what is right to a particular outcome, perspective, or decision. Rigid thinking disallows more than one "right" way. A stretch for Ones is to see multiple perspectives as valid. Different perspectives bring different gifts and possibilities.

The defense mechanism of reaction formation supports the image of one who is good. When this defense mechanism is in play, Ones will judge as wrong an action or decision they wish they could do or make themselves. An example of this is the type One who gets angry at their partner who is sitting on the sofa reading the newspaper instead of engaging in or helping with a task. The One in this situation wants to be reading the paper too, but believes that the responsible and right thing to do is to remain on task. Resentment builds, anger arrives, and the partner is seen as irresponsible. The inner One in us all can benefit from considering, *"When is it wrong to be responsible?"*

In my work with Ones in type groups and in individual spiritual direction sessions, I've noticed their desire to grow and devotion to engaging in practices enabling them to do so. When Ones stay steady and present to themselves, their tenacity sharpens their focus inward. More than once, I've witnessed their transformation in the moment, whether from anger to serenity or from self-criticism to self-acceptance. Ones' dedication to their growth is inspiring.

The Core Fear and the Pivot

Within Ones is an unconscious false belief and core avoidance that "I am inherently wrong." This false narrative drives Ones to believe that

"My right to be in the world and my goodness hinge on my earning it." They *must* engage in good works. They *must* be good people. It seems to Ones that they can never be good enough. This narrative is at the root of Ones' fear of making mistakes, as well as Ones' inability to separate themselves from the mistake. When they make a mistake, Ones can believe they *are* the mistake. Mistakes stay a while, taking up residence in the mind as the inner critic continues its ranting. For this reason, critical feedback is difficult to hear. Realizing this can guide us to a **compassionate entry point**, supporting Ones as they shift from a sense of wrongness to acceptance.

With an inner critic giving endless monologues about missteps and errors made, "good enough" is a difficult place to land. So, Ones achieve, stay on task, improving and completing. Then the cycle begins again. Some of the last words my grandmother, a self-preserving One herself, said to me were, "Sandra, it pays to be busy!" When relating to Ones, ask questions rather than pointing out the faux pas. Abstain from comments like "That was inappropriate" or "I think you're wrong on this." Instead, ask a question: "Is there another way to approach this?"

When the fear of being wrong is strong, it blinds Ones to their inherent goodness and beauty. Yet, inherent goodness resides in all of us, with no need to earn it. When Ones relax into their own goodness, the striving to be good ceases. Goodness simply flows. Serenity, the virtue of this type, brings a contentment, a knowing that nothing needs to be improved. Fear of wrongness dissolves as Ones realize that their notion of earning is needless busy work.

Ones: *Accepting what is in this moment opens you to your heart's compassion. Your dreams and desires surface when your heart leads. Acceptance and joy do not require earning.*

Companion Voices

As you read the stories from the companion writers, be open to finding a part of you in their shared experiences.

Our first type One contributor, **Claudia**, describes paths to spontaneity and curiosity as she claims being "One-derful." Embracing both/and thinking is a grace-filled path.

I am a Latina, brown-skinned, middle-aged woman who has enjoyed careers in education, politics, and most recently, ministry. I scoffed at the idea of engaging with the Enneagram. I didn't want to be defined by a type. When a professional development workshop revealed that I engage as a One, I wondered if someone had been following me around and taking notes. Organized, list-maker, diplomatic, thorough, self-disciplined, feeling obligated to improve myself and the world . . . it was me! And the shadow side too—opinionated, impatient, rigid, perfectionistic, judgmental, critical, and self-critical. Wow! Reading about my Enneagram type was a confirmation of things I knew about myself and an invitation to reflect on how those tendencies have guided me through rewarding and fulfilling experiences as well as times of struggle and deep disappointment. For example, in 2016, those gifts kept me focused as I juggled divinity school, work, and my final year as an elected school board member. And at the same time, perfectionism and rigidity led to anxiety and tension in my relationships as I multitasked and refused to accept "good enough" when completing work projects and grad school assignments.

After three years of exploring the Enneagram, I am more aware of my tendencies and know that I can interrupt them. I can look back and see how my strengths and weaknesses have shaped who I am today. I have learned that I am not defined by my One-ness. Knowing about my vices and virtues, mental fixations, and blind spots has challenged me to embrace my whole self with greater compassion. There can be joy in my One-derfulness. And I can also be intentional about exploring the shadow side of One, knowing that I can make choices about how I am in the world and the stories I tell myself about myself. I can be flexibly scheduled, realistically compassionate, and joyfully reliable. I can stop working before everything is complete. What a concept! My rigidity and high expectations blinded me to that possibility. I know how committed and hardworking I am. Now, if everything on my to-do list doesn't get done in my workday, it's okay, and I am okay.

My intensity, fueled by passion, has been an asset in my political and ministerial work. And these qualities have also been deleterious when not tempered. How can I temper myself? I've learned to be more vulnerable and less intense by exploring improv and art in group settings. Improv and art challenge me be open to delight and lightness as I play with words, scenarios, and color, creating art or scenes for fun, rather than for public display. Improv has also been a fun way of releasing the need to know and prepare in advance. There is no way of knowing what one's scene partner is going to say, so responses cannot be rehearsed. I am expected to respond in the moment with no time for crafting the perfect response. That was very scary, at first!

The improv "yes, and" concept helped me to move from black-and-white thinking to a more spacious awareness of the gray areas in life. By shifting to a "yes, and" approach, I felt a shift in conversations as I acknowledged what was said (without seeming judgmental) and added my thoughts on the matter for their consideration. That was transformative for me. As a minister, I am in the improv business every day. Unexpected invitations to say a few words, unexpected pastoral care conversations . . . I can't prepare the perfect words for those moments. Rather, I trust my experiences and the wisdom I have acquired in my lifetime, and I get present in my body. I am always grounding, listening, and improvising.

Also, I have learned to lessen my judging mind by embracing curiosity. I have been setting the intention each morning to engage in wonder and curiosity before moving to reactivity and judgment. I don't always remember, but I am noticing that there are times when curiosity leads, and it does make a difference. Wonder and curiosity open up conversations. Reactivity closes doors. On automatic, I react and respond without thinking about the implications of my words. When I finally stop talking and get curious, I consider how I could have handled myself more compassionately. This awareness of my tendencies and intentionality about shifting patterns of behavior has been a gift from engaging with the Enneagram.

Exploring anger through the lens of the Enneagram has also been transformative. I have learned that when anger arises, I've deprived myself of something I wanted. Or it may stem from my expectations and frustration when things aren't the way I think they should be. *Then I project my expectations of perfection and self-sacrifice onto others.* My attitude of "If I can do it, they can do it" makes it difficult to allow space for different approaches and priorities in the lives of people I work with and people I care about. Being aware of that dynamic has been helpful. When I sense that frustration rising, I remember why I love and/or appreciate the person I am interacting with. Again, that tempers the often reflexive impulse to judge them.

Exploring the Enneagram has invited me to think about how much my type One tendencies have been influenced by my immigration experience. As a child, witnessing the treatment of my parents and myself as "less than" because we are Latiné pushed me to want to do whatever it took to fit in; to work hard and get it right; to prove that I belonged. My parents had high expectations of us because they came to the United States so we could have a better life, go to college, and be successful. Plowing through three college degrees was one way of earning my worth. Multitasking and being on boards, running for office, working full-time and caring for my family—well, they all had to be done perfectly! It has taken me years to let go of that mindset and recognize that I have worth without needing to prove it to anyone. My yearly Enneagram workshops have been a safe place to review my life story and shift the narrative to a more affirming, compassionate way of being and seeing myself. It has been a gift to connect with other type One women with whom I can relate and who are on the journey of knowing ourselves better so we can live to our potential and be a force for love in the world. Our One-ness provides a common ground that creates openness and reminds me that I am not bound by my type.

Claudia's move to engage in improv is a courageous act. Typically, Ones shy away from spontaneity. Perhaps transformation for Ones is simply dropping the "e" on improve and shifting to improv!

I appreciate how Claudia understands the Enneagram as an invitation to see herself more clearly, rather than seeing her type as a restriction. Understanding a type One's striving through the lens of an immigrant wanting to fit in brings my compassion forward.

In this next contribution, **Frederica** shares her struggles with judgment and her inner critic along with her liberating work of embodiment.

At my parents' recent 50th anniversary party, while I was chatting idly with some guests and sipping champagne, an older gentleman approached me. Let's call him Mustache, due to the impressive handlebar whiskers protruding four inches out on either side of his face. Evidently in response to comments I had made in my toast earlier that evening, Mustache demanded that I defend my support for the Black Lives Matter movement. "More Black people kill each other than are killed by police," he argued, adding that he'd supported Martin Luther

King in the '60s and was therefore not racist. And, finally, for good measure, he stated that today's "cancel culture" was no different than the fascism of the Nazis and of North Korea. His opening salvo complete, he stood there expectantly, awaiting my rebuttal. But I just gaped at him, frozen, baffled, and tongue-tied. My whole body had shifted into stress mode: leg muscles tense, heart rate elevated, mind inconveniently clouded over, and the rage that I normally keep tamped down simmering up at the surface. I stammered out something dismissive, awkwardly changed the subject, and at the soonest opportunity extracted myself from the conversation.

This encounter with Mustache was not my first opportunity to engage a fellow white person in a conversation about race. And it was definitely not the first time that I had utterly failed to skillfully and completely convert my conversation partner into a repentant, enlightened, racial justice crusader, which is actually what I expect of myself in those moments. The truth is, as a white cisgender woman dominant in type One, my journey of learning to take ownership of my participation in the oppressive system of white supremacy has also been a journey of working with the challenges that present uniquely to Enneagram Ones.

As a One, my ego works very hard to maintain the idea that I am a good person, but especially a good *white* woman—a valuable ally, an active anti-racist. It is not uncommon for me to feel inherently wrong when it comes to race work, and I can overcompensate by trying to be extra pious and good. I hold myself and other white people to an impossibly high standard of being exemplary anti-racists in every single moment. When I fail, my shame runs deep, and when others fail, I judge them harshly. I am often afraid of doing or saying the wrong thing, so my anti-racism work takes on perfectionism, and this exacerbates white fragility. White fragility, which is really fear, is therefore especially strong in me, and especially dangerous because it can so easily cause me to shut down and run away, as I did in my conversation with Mustache.

I have worked to move beyond my core inner belief from childhood that I am inherently wrong, but what do we white Ones do when confronted with the harsh truth that our deeply internalized white supremacy is real and runs deep? How do I integrate this into my own spiritual work of nonjudgmental self-acceptance? Not easily. After more than 20 years of racism trainings, Diversity, Equity, and Inclusion committee work, marches, activism, and self-work around white supremacy and white privilege, I still wallow in the notion that I am not ally enough, not woke enough, and that there is still so far to go. Even confessing this can be performative for Ones: "Look at my self-flagellation! I must be really woke and aware to feel this bad. And if I feel badly enough, you'll see that I'm really good."

The path forward begins in an unexpected place for me: embodiment work. When someone asks me where in my body I sense something, I'm usually stumped. My body senses things? I have very recently begun to wake up, like a child, to the vast world of information and intelligence available to me from my body. Like many white people and many Ones, I am not accustomed to honoring my raw impulses and animal instincts, or listening to the wisdom of my body. But lately I have been pausing to listen. I have been carving out little bits of unstructured time for play and for pleasure. On a recent Saturday, I wandered around trails in the woods nearby with no destination and no agenda. I just was. I have been sitting down to join my young daughters in make-believe play, and I am cultivating and honoring erotic energy as vital to my everyday life. This is necessary for anti-racism work because I carry the intergenerational and historical trauma of white supremacy in my body; it is where I house my shame, sadness, and grief. I believe that we all need to feel the depth of racism *in our bodies* to know more completely what we are feeling and sensing, so that transformation, when it happens, can be complete.

Perhaps most reassuring of all for me, surprisingly, has been to sit with and accept the possibility that I am inherently and irredeemably racist, meaning I am complicit in structures of racial injustice. I find unexpected comfort in the notion that white people just can't get it right. I am learning to dwell in this grey area, this nondual reality, this uncomfortable place of accepting the imperfect in me, and then in others, in Mustache, and in the world around me. Holy Perfection is the enlightened spiritual perspective of a One, and when I move toward it, I stop striving so hard to be right and good, and allow my goodness to simply flow. While I still see the imperfection everywhere—there's no turning that off—I do see it as perfect in its own way. *Imperfect is the new perfect*, I tell myself. I begin to know that there is nothing fundamentally wrong with me because I am a part of everything. Turns out the salvation of the world doesn't depend on me. Racial justice advocate Layla Saad says, "I don't care about perfectionism. I care about truth, because truth sets us free and makes us better." Removing perfection from the table makes space for raw honesty.

After extracting myself from the conversation with Mustache, I maneuvered back to my table and plunked myself down next to my older brother, seething with annoyance and self-loathing. I told him about the exchange briefly, and it prompted him to tell me about the fumbling journey into anti-racism work that he and his frisbee team had embarked on during the summer of 2020 in response to the BLM uprisings. I listened. He was vulnerable, and so was I. He asked questions, and I offered responses based on what rose up from within my body rather than memorized talking points. I pointed out, lovingly, how white fragility was showing up for both of us in this work, and how hard but important the work still is. In that conversation with my brother, I was still striving for raising consciousnesses in both of us, but it came from a place of self-love and love for him rather than a place of striving or of proving something. The conversation was not perfect. I don't think he walked away from it radically transformed. I will continue to have imperfect conversations about race, but I will bring my full, embodied presence into those conversations—and this, I believe, is how my real goodness shows up.

Ones often report not being in touch with their body's sensations and wisdom. Frederica offers a glimpse into the body's role in One's justice-making and leading with compassion. Her shift to owning and accepting her own and the world's imperfection through her embodiment work is core for Ones.

Alchemy: From Type to Essence

Holy Perfection as Enlightened Spiritual Perspective

Serenity, the virtue of Ones, brings peace in each moment. All is well. In the company of serenity, the vice of anger recedes, as does the judging mind. A state of acceptance sees the "is-ness" of now and celebrates what is without the need to reform, order, or tidy up. Acceptance offers Ones the space to rest in a world that is simultaneously chaotic and beautiful. Holy Perfection!

Accepting is a loving heart's response to life—to self and other. The heart has no need or desire to evaluate; this is the mind's need. Evaluation implies standards, and the landscape of the heart is absent of standards. There is no dividing line between right and wrong. When Ones journey to the wisdom of the heart, their deeper selves offer a serenity that calms. Mistakes become a part of life's learning, endearing Ones more to themselves and to others. Asking for and receiving what they want brings more balance into life. Resentments fade when the self is remembered and accepted. When seen through the eye of the heart, the world is a feast of order and Holy Perfection.

PRACTICES Bringing Awareness to Ones' Core Issues

Focused Inquiry

+ *What is between you and self-acceptance right now?*
+ *What do you sacrifice in your life in order to complete tasks?*
+ *When has improving been a barrier to your loving fully?*
+ *How might connecting with spontaneity be a gateway to self-acceptance?*

Our practices are ways of saying "yes" to our journey to our Essence.

Engagement to Counter the Type's Patterns

+ Discern what really is your responsibility and what is another's. Stay in your lane!
+ Notice when "should" enters your thinking. What's driving the "should"? Are there other options or right ways?
+ Recall a moment when you made a mistake and didn't lose yourself. How did you separate yourself from the mistake? Stay with the memory and the feeling.
+ When you feel the intensity of a serious tone, add a measure of lightheartedness and feel both.
+ Take time to ask about your heart's desires and find ways to fulfill those. Ask yourself *"What makes my heart sing?"* and do that.

- Routinely stop before a task is done. Breathe into the anxiety that may arise and trust that your thinking will be more creative when you later return to the task.
- Own playfulness without hiding it behind duty or feeling you have to earn it. See reading, gardening, and other activities you enjoy as play. It is right for Ones to relax and play.

Ones benefit from a practice of Sabbath, a day of cultivating delight. No lists, no responsibilities, and no guilt. This is restorative and brings balance to an overly busy life.

BEYOND YOUR TYPE

In the eyes of acceptance, you relax into your inner goodness. Wrong and right no longer exist. All is inherently perfect without effort to improve.

Sabbath-Keeping

Sabbath, in the traditional Jewish understanding, directs our focus to awe and provides space for us to cultivate delight in creation and our lives. Sabbath invites us to wake up to ourselves and our world.

This day's rhythm is that of a "demandless" day, giving a rest to the inner critic. Ones often feel controlled by time, and there is never enough time for both work and play. Resentment arises from constant duty to the "ought tos" and depriving the self of the "want tos."

Sabbath is a day for pleasure—no responsibilities, and no guilt for the lack of responsibilities during this day. There are no emails to respond to and no phone calls to make. What fun activity have you been wanting to do but putting off? Ask someone to help you do or get what you want. (Requesting this can be difficult for Ones, who think of themselves as the "responsible adult.") What would please you? Staying in bed all day with a book and a cup of tea may be just the right thing for you (even if the sun is shining!). When the feeling of "slacking off" arises, it's a sign you're on the right path!

Experience the "soft animal" of your body as natural and free, rather than out of control. Notice what feels good to your body today. Be tactile. Allow your instinctual energy to emerge, and feel its inherent goodness. Throw caution to the wind! Welcome disorder. There is no wrong way today. Practice celebration by naming that which is good in your life.

And finally, allow your Sabbath to be a time to cultivate awe. Awe allows us to yield to the flow of life rather than opposing it, helping us to cultivate acceptance for what is. In this state of wonder and acceptance we can sense the inherent perfection in creation and in ourselves, and realize there is nothing to improve or to resist.

A Type One Prayer

May I hold myself in this perfect moment, loving me because of who I am, not in spite of who I am. I now empty myself of judgments and guilt as I relax into the awe and wonder of life. In self-acceptance, I loosen rules and lower standards that prevent me from fully loving. Ground of Being, teach me forgiveness, so that I may forgive myself for not forgiving myself. May I come to know my inherent goodness, deep in my marrow, so that my efforts lessen and my joy arises. May I rest in the boundless grace and mercy that surrounds me and holds me.

Heart Types
Three, Two, Four

First Way of Knowing: Tone, feeling, mood

Primary Emotional Issue: Grief, shame

Orientation: Quality connections

Energy: Engaging or over-engaging

Sensitivity: Being unlovable

Growth: Claiming self-worth

CHAPTER 7

The Power of Being: Type Three

All of us, without realizing it, work to support an image of ourselves, how we want others to see us. This image is intimately tied to the ego ideal's small story of us. Because people who lead with type Three are particularly invested in how others see them, they are continually shifting their image in order to look better in others' eyes. Who others want them to be has greater importance than who they want to become, until more inner awareness develops. "Who am I in my own eyes?" is a good inquiry for us all. As you read this chapter, invite the type Three within you to listen in.

TYPE THREE AT A GLANCE

Strengths: Engages easily, competent, executes and implements
Ego Ideal: I am accomplished.
Focus of Attention: Tasks to do
Motivation: To accomplish and be recognized
Worldview: The world is a competitive arena where you win or lose.
Fixation: Vanity
Vice: Deceit
Holy Idea: Holy Hope
Virtue: Honesty

Brief Overview

Threes are upbeat, optimistic, and competent. When away from tasks, they offer a lightness at gatherings, whether at work or socially, making them fun companions and colleagues. Rarely do they seem disgruntled, and they consistently display an even temperament. Others appreciate Threes' reliability and efficiency. They are inspirational in their ability to get things done and support us in accomplishing more than we realized we could.

The Three's focus of attention is on tasks and producing results. A performance-driven life has few pauses, and the fast pace serves as a barrier to Threes' emotional life and to deepening relationships. The underlying belief is that emotions get in the way of doing, thus emotions remain fuzzy unknown entities in the background. The task list becomes the "beloved" as Threes find juiciness in task completion and checking things off the list. Claudio Naranjo named this type *ego-go*—and how true that is! Whether the list is mental or material, Threes are constantly *moving through it and adding to it.* Completing a task and crossing it off the list is affirming for this type. We all know how good we feel when we mark off a "to do" item on our list. This good feeling is a bit of an addiction for Threes ... until an external or internal force invites them (or knocks them) off the hamster wheel and into a still point. In this stillness, Threes can relax into their exquisite being.

Putting their best foot forward is image-bound when Threes believe that they have no choice. No humans can be their best selves all of the time. The vice of deceit means that Threes confuse their authentic selves with the image they present. They easily shapeshift to fit the image they believe others desire, and they disconnect emotionally to support that image. As the center of the heart triad, Threes have great capacity for heart connections. They need only to slow their quick pace, linger in those moments of connection, allow emotions to arise, and know themselves as lovable. In continuing their fast and efficient way of doing, Threes outrun their hearts.

During a guest interview on the *Heart of the Enneagram* podcast that I co-host with my colleague Christopher Copeland, we asked our Three guest Drew Jones how he knew the difference between his image-crafting and his authentic self. Drew said, "I notice my face. Am I smiling when I don't feel like it?" Other indicators that Threes are in performance mode are a constricted body and minimal breathing. They may freeze their breath in the chest area while simultaneously experiencing confidence and a powerful "buzz." The impressing and the doing impede Threes from being who they really are and who they want to become. More than other types, Threes are invested in projecting a favorable self-image. They wear a role well. This is a gift, because there are times when our culture needs people to wear the mantle of a role well. The challenge comes when Threes get stuck in the role and can't discern themselves from it. "Know thyself," not just the presentation. If you lead with Three, inquire throughout the day, *Am I being genuine right now? What tells me this?*

The Striving and the Avoidance

A fear of failure is to be avoided, so Threes strive to accomplish, succeed, and impress, adhering to the ego ideal of this type ("I am accomplished"). The illusion that time is for producing keeps Threes on the fast track to avoid failing. When this fear is strong, it blinds Threes to the gifts of simply being. Efficiency rules the day, making relaxing and relating more difficult. What I call the "syndrome of the separate doer" evolves as those who lead with this type begin to believe that if tasks are to get done, they must be the ones to accomplish them. The self in relation to the whole is replaced with the separate self, the separate doer. *It's all up to me!* Sooner or later, Threes get the sense that working is a form of relaxing because doing alleviates anxiety. This is a false notion that supports continued doing. Threes decide and implement fast. They can be impatient with others who spend time thinking and feeling, and they can become reactive when forward progress is thwarted by those with questions and options. The fear of *being seen as inept* is a greater motivator than the drive to succeed. Threes easily move into a self-perception of being the one at fault, the one who failed. Being aware of this propensity in Threes gives us a **compassionate entry point** when our beloved Threes feel this sense of disappointment in others' eyes.

Quick forward movement suppresses feelings. Though it is possible to weave emotions into our doing, impressing and feeling rarely coexist. When any of us are in the mode of impressing, we are suppressing emotions. Impressing does not engage the heart. The drive to impress and do blinds Threes to what they really want for themselves. A good practice for Threes is to take time alone with no list. This creates space to allow emotions to surface and to relate to the heart. *What is your heart's desire? How do you truly define success?*

The defense mechanism for Threes is identification. Identifying with or emulating someone they see as successful strengthens their idealized image of themselves and creates a barrier to knowing the genuine self. Threes step into a role so fully that their inner life recedes as the "winning" image takes center stage. The view of the world as a competitive arena nudges Threes to be seen as a winner, to be in good standing in the eyes of others. This raises the question, *"Who are you in your own eyes?"*

The Core Fear and the Pivot

Threes form their identity through their activities and performance. "I do; therefore, I am loved." Threes' core fear is visceral and seems real: "What if I really am loved for what I do?" This fear drives the constant doing. Whether conscious or not, at the core of Threes' fear is a false belief that "I can't accomplish"; therefore, I won't be loved. The more prominent this false belief becomes, the more active Threes are. A Three pattern is to stay up late working on tasks and to rise early to begin working on them again. In the mind of Threes, ceasing activity means that love abandons them. We all want to be known, recognized, and loved. When we believe we may not be, we grasp for love in type-specific ways. Within every Three is a *sensitivity to being unlovable*. This lies at the core of the striving to do whatever will evoke love and approval from others.

Understanding this reveals a **compassionate entry point** for those who love Threes. To name and to demonstrate that your love for them isn't related to their doing is a gift. However, this isn't as easy as it seems. How can we relay our love to Threes when their filters are so skewed toward *doing equals love*? This is a worthy conversation to have with our beloved Threes.

An underlying sadness develops over time from rejecting the authentic self. Over-doing is a sure sign that such feelings are just below the surface and in need of attention. Recognizing these times of over-doing and *pivoting to non-doing* will create anxiety and is an avenue to growth. This is a courageous moment for Threes. Breathing through and staying with the anxiety, without judgment, eventually brings a steadiness. Dropping beneath the roles and anxiety, Threes have a pathway to their hearts. An honesty emerges on this path that shines a light on the grand deception that equates love with doing. Here, in the stillness of the heart, the beauty of their being radiates and Threes know, beyond a shadow of a doubt, that they are not their performance.

Threes: *The path to connection and love opens when you relax into the* *knowing that you are a part of the whole. Successes and failures are not singular acts or moments by an individual. We are in this together.*

Companion Voices

As you read the stories from the companion writers, be open to finding a part of you in their shared experiences.

Stillness is good practice as it brings us to a place of choice: repeat my patterns or travel a new path. **Cyndi,** our next contributor, speaks to the powerful pairing of using the Enneagram Map and engaging in a practice that counters the patterns of her type.

When I heard someone say that Ennea-type Threes complete tasks as a form of relaxation, I finally felt absolutely certain about my dominant type. My mouth actually fell open. How could someone know this about me when I didn't know it about myself until it was spoken out loud? As soon as the words were in the air, I could see this truth. Yes! To me, it's relaxing to cross out a couple more items from my list, cook up a feast, or organize and clean. It feels a bit shameful to own this truth, because I know it sounds a little crazy to some.

And, it helps me understand why meditation has been such a life-changing practice for me. As I reflect, I see that I delved deeply into the Enneagram and began practicing meditation in earnest at the same time, when I went through two year-long trainings—yoga teacher training, followed by a certification course to become a professional coach who works with leaders and changemakers.

Prior to this period of awakening, my world reflected many hallmarks of a typical Three. I secured multiple degrees, earned promotions and took on greater responsibility in every workplace, beamed "success" in my marriage and home life, kept all the plates spinning . . . and paid very little attention to how I felt. I was proud to be a white woman taking on issues of social responsibility in the civic sphere through devotion to educational reform and advocacy for libraries. These mantles were an important part of my identity. I thought doing *was* being.

Although meditation was immediately beneficial, it took about two years for me to understand *why* it had such a powerful impact on my way of being, my experience of life. I had to learn more about the Enneagram first.

For 10 months, I proceeded with the notion that I led with Enneagram type Two. I felt quite sure that I was a compassionate helper. Eventually, I came to understand that although I am strongly flavored by type Two, the typical Two strengths described how I *wanted* to be seen, how I wanted to see myself. Identifying with type Two was easier than "admitting" my Threeness.

I do not consider those months as time wasted. (And there it is—a type Three's characteristic focus on efficiency!) To a degree, I *have* defined who I am by being of service, so exploring type Two was useful territory. Who am I when I'm not helping? What is the right amount to give, and when? My foray into type Two revealed that we have spoonfuls of each type within us—sometimes many spoonfuls! Studying *each* Enneagram type helps me grow more conscious.

My deeper awakening to type Three came as a result of a conversation with a leadership coach who worked with the Enneagram. She asked me some discerning questions, like, "Is it more important to you to feel *liked* or *respected*?" When I realized that being respected was more important to me, it opened up my understanding of the type Three worldview, a limiting belief that the world is a competitive place, and I must perform and achieve.

I pivoted my focus to seeing the type Three within. Through self-observation and reflection, I came to see my motivation to garner respect through being competent and impressive. I noticed and allowed myself to feel a sense of shame when others did not reflect approval. I started to pay attention to my emotions. Blind spots became less blind.

Big new ideas opened up, like: *"I am inherently valuable NOW and always. I do not need to earn love through accomplishing great things."* and *"I have needs and feelings to tend, and others want to know what I struggle with as well as what successes I experience."*

Fireworks went off in my head, my heart, my belly as I let these realizations sink in over time.

Meanwhile, I was meditating most days. I believe I was developing my inner observer both on and off the cushion. As I practiced meditation, I learned to sit with reality, taking a witness orientation. I grew my capacity to *just be*, to hold whatever showed up in each moment. I visualized myself as an empty vessel—grounded, expanding.

Somatically, I became conscious of aligning my ears, shoulders, and hips—lifting my chest and fully inhabiting myself. I could sense when my head, heart, and body centers felt aligned.

In one particularly potent meditation, the image of a silver lightsaber appeared, and I sensed energy zap into life as each of my centers "turned on." The lightsaber image has stayed with me for years now, and when it shows up, I feel a sense of living as pure awareness. I often receive an immediate sense of "right action" if I've been holding a question.

It's difficult for me to admit that doing twice as many tasks as other Enneagram types might do in a day feels absolutely normal to me. At one point, I might have taken pride in my busyness and ability to get sh*t done. But learning about the Enneagram changed that. I'll never forget when, at an Enneagram course, a person who led with type Nine came up to me after I had participated in a panel with other Threes. He said, "As I listened to you share on that panel, I felt absolutely exhausted." He did not say this with malice. He was just reflecting his own experience, and his truth helped me see myself through someone else's eyes more clearly.

That experience came in handy recently.

It's been years now that I've been tempering my overused strengths of abundant energy and competence, and I still have opportunities to do so. Lately, I had been reflecting on and celebrating my progress with moving at a slower, more spacious pace. In particular, I was feeling very steady from my meditation and mindful awareness practice. So, I was quite taken aback when my husband blurted out one night, "You're zooming around like you're on some kind of drug." Ouch! How painful it felt to recognize that my "slower speed" felt that fast to him!

Though painful, it took me less time to notice my emotion, see from his perspective, and regain my equilibrium. The next day, I was able to speak calmly, state my feelings, and ask for what I needed . . . *and* hold the feeling of shame with compassion for myself.

This is "waking up," in my experience. I want to be awake, and the Enneagram has helped me awaken. Although it's an important first step, just learning to *see* the Three type structure at work is not enough. Thank goodness I took on the simultaneous practice of learning how to meet each moment with mindful awareness, to see myself as part of consciousness, to disidentify with my smaller self of egoic patterns.

Meditation strengthens my ability to see my Threeness with more curiosity, less judgment. It reinforces one of the most powerful and elegant invitations of the Enneagram: to pause. And in that pause, to remember I have the ability to pivot instead of reacting in habitual ways. Dancing with the necessity of ego and the remembrance of Essence is never-ending. I'm grateful to be one who is dancing, and also one who is standing in the balcony, witnessing the moves with love.

Our inner observer plays a foundational role in our transformation. Creating more internal spaciousness to witness ourselves as both dancer and observer, as Cyndi says, is the gateway to growth—when we hold ourselves in our loving hearts.

Now we shift to a narrative form of expression as **Celeste** shares her experience of having breast cancer. She speaks to the patterns of Threes as she navigated her new reality.

"You didn't bring anyone with you?" the receptionist at the breast imaging center asked.

"Excuse me?" I responded.

"For your appointment, are you alone?" (Awkward pause.) I nodded. I was, in fact, alone.

"Wow, I guess I have breast cancer," I said to her in disbelief. She wouldn't make eye contact as she mumbled a reply. I went to sit in the lobby, my mind racing.

I'd been there the week before (December 19, 2013). Then, as the doctor inserted the biopsy needle, he called the tissue an "architectural abnormality," without defined edges, not cancer.

"Shouldn't we wait on the pathology report?" I asked.

"You can if you want, but it's not cancer," he stated confidently. I relaxed into his certainty, thankful to put the worry out of my mind and to enjoy the Christmas holiday with family and friends.

A week later, I was back for the follow-up appointment. Since the doctor had said it wasn't cancer, I'd come alone, in the trance of my type Three patterns, efficiency the goal. Get in. Confirm the good news. Get out. Check it off my list and go on to the next post-Christmas task.

Breast cancer is in my family—lots of it. So much that I never questioned *if* I would get breast cancer, only *when*. Yearly mammograms had been part of my routine for over a decade. My plan: catch cancer early, conquer it, move on. My mammogram in April had been "clear," but at my annual checkup the doctor had found a suspicious area and sent me for another mammogram that led to the biopsy that I was waiting to hear about.

Alone, I waited in the lobby. Stunned. This cannot be real.

It was real. Very real. Left mastectomy. Chemo. Drugs. Continuing to work. Bald head. Pain. Radiation. Still working. Fatigue. Chest expander. Reconstruction implant surgery. And the scar that did not heal.

Fast forward—August 7, 2015: The plastic surgeon determined that the implant would have to be removed. The radiated breast tissue simply would not heal. I tried to come to terms with what had happened and what lay ahead.

Before the reconstruction surgery, I'd felt terrific. I was ready to get my new breast implant, recover, and work on issues that had been weighing on my heart—racial healing, economic justice, and equality for those who identify as LGBTQIA+.

But the scar didn't heal. Instead, more doctor's appointments, antibiotics, stitches, and on and on . . .

All those surgeries and nothing to show for it! After the extraction, I'd essentially be where I would have been without reconstruction.

If I hadn't chosen reconstruction, I would have been FINISHED a YEAR ago: my last radiation treatment.

Was this my fault? I was sure that something about *me*—after all the cancer shit I'd endured, survived, conquered—had caused this "epic fail." Regardless of how many times the surgeon said there was nothing I could've done differently, I spent hours replaying the days up to and after the implant surgery. Was I not careful enough? Was I incapable of "taking it easy?" Should I have only slept on my back? Eaten more protein? Exercised less? My inner Three voice was relentless, creating the duality of success or failure and shouting the illusion that "it's all up to me."

Why did the thought of not having a left breast make me feel "less than?" On this emotional roller coaster, I got mad about how messed up it is that so much self-esteem and self-worth can be tangled up in these bulging slabs of flesh and mammary glands, even after they've served their purpose for nursing babies. When did I buy into that societal message that "woman = two breasts" and the more dangerous message that "gorgeous, vibrant, vital woman = two *perky* breasts?" On some level, I must have believed it, to have put myself through the reconstruction ordeal! How did I get so brainwashed?

Extraction: Friday, 7:45 a.m., plastic surgeon's office for the implant removal surgery. Lots of medication. I don't remember that day.

The scar: Late Saturday night, when everyone was in bed, I took off the bandage. I wasn't prepared for what I saw. It took my breath away: not the flat, straight scar that I'd expected. Instead, the tissue was lumpy, folded over, swirls of skin wrinkled around a deep, purple cavern where the implant had been. The drain tube protruded through my skin into an opaque, plastic bulb pinned to the surgical bra. I looked in the mirror in disbelief. Nothing on the internet showed such disfigurement, scars so misshapen and grotesque. I realized I would see this scar every day I looked in the mirror, every shower, every time I changed clothes, for the rest of my life.

Despair: The days following the surgery were some of the darkest, hardest, and saddest I can remember. I was depleted from months of struggle, working to reframe hard things, thinking I could beat this, trying to keep a positive outlook. And I was so, so sad. Sad to see my poor, disfigured, mutilated chest; the folds of skin and bulging tissue looked like *Star Wars'* Jabba the Hut had taken up residence on my chest. My image of being whole and healthy, feminine and worthy— now gone. Who am I now?

Why bother? I cried a lot, wondering why it had ended so badly. Why was I even trying to find light, hope, and encouragement? Since December 19, 2013, every time I thought I'd made it through, something else had happened. I was sad and numb. My body was on high alert all the time. It was hard to eat or sleep. When I finally slept, the pain in my left arm from my frozen shoulder would wake me up. I kept trying to rally emotionally, telling myself that at least I didn't have cancer; it was "only" a failed implant that left a hideous scar. But after all the struggle, pain, confusion, uncertainty, stress, and expense it felt like so much more . . . the last straw, the final blow. I'd lost the will to put on my happy, hopeful "I've got this" face. Gone was my desire to be the breast cancer super shero; I withdrew to figure out how to deal with my new reality.

Follow-up: At my one-week check up with the plastic surgeon, I conveyed how unprepared I'd been for the horrible scar. I even offered to give the doctor pictures of my scar to prepare other women who have failed implants removed. The doctor was kind and understanding as I talked and cried for a long time. She reassured me that there was nothing that I'd done to cause the implant to fail; it is very difficult for radiated tissue to heal. She said the extraction scar looked good and called attention to extra skin that she'd left in case I wanted to try reconstruction again. I looked at her like she had lost her mind. *"Not just no, but hell no! Why would I put myself through this AGAIN? Just to* *have a breast? Am I the only one who thinks that is absolute insanity after what I've been through?"*

Down to the River to Pray: After the appointment, I sought refuge in nature: the French Broad River Park full of memories of walks with the kids when they were little and just learning to ride bikes, with our dog Angel who passed away in 2013, by myself, with friends. I sat by the river and cried out to God. I grieved, questioned, and prayed. Vividly Jesus came to me, like in the scriptures when he went to the wounded, diseased, condemned, and outcast. He looked at me and my scar with love and acceptance. He was with me, then and there, in my pain and sorrow. With him I saw that the scar represented the struggle I'd endured; it isn't beautiful as our culture defines beauty, but it did nothing to diminish me as a child of God in whom God takes great delight. That moment by the river, held in Jesus' tender, redeeming, and accepting love, was a turning point for me. I was, I am, beloved. And the Light began to overtake the darkness.

Beauty in imperfection: In the natural world, I am blessed and sustained by the beautiful flowers, plants, and wildlife—often snapping pictures of them in all their glory. Outside, alone, is where I break away from being driven by tasks and accomplishments. It's where I challenge myself to be in the moment, to breathe deeply, to quiet internal voices of judgment and feel divine love and acceptance.

Surviving—a decade later: During the hellscape of breast cancer, daily walks brought me peace and healing. They still do. Immersed in nature, I am awed by creation—often snapping pictures of blossoms, bark, birds, rivers, rocks, ridges, moss, mushrooms, and mountain vistas in all their glory. Perfect? No. Beautiful? Yes! I breathe deeply to quiet internal voices of judgment and feel divine love and acceptance. My chest and prosthetic breast are daily reminders that my scarred body doesn't measure up to society's depictions of beauty. I refuse to let my physical imperfections diminish me. I AM ALIVE for all that life offers: loss and love, pain and joy, sickness and health, darkness and LIGHT . . . and everything in between!

Imperfection can be woven into an image of beauty, as Celeste suggests. Imperfection can be held without judgment in the loving heart. When Threes stand on this Ground, they are the teachers for us in Hope, formed in the honesty that reveals that all belongs— even the scars. Both of these Three contributors spoke to spiritual practice and faith as a bedrock, a part of their inner foundation. *What is your bedrock?*

Alchemy: From Type to Essence

Holy Hope as Enlightened Spiritual Perspective

Our culture often seems removed from its heart, and this creates an overlay on all of us to live in ways that distance ourselves from our emotions. Busyness gives us a sense of importance, seducing us away from our hearts. When we avoid our hearts, our discernment turns to judgment, compassion to reaction, and fear overshadows love.

In the turn from deception to honesty, Threes begin to understand the relationship between love and being. Seeing themselves through the eyes of the heart brings tenderness and acceptance, allowing Threes to deepen their inner exploration. In their depths, they find the treasure of their Ground of Being. Solid and steady, quiet and strong, this Ground gives hope. Holy Hope comes with the understanding that Threes aren't alone. They are woven into life's seamless web, where each action is felt and known by all. Hope comes when the striving to accomplish dissolves. This is the grand accomplishment for Threes: stillness, the gateway to love.

PRACTICES Bringing Awareness to Threes' Core Issues

Focused Inquiry

+ *How do you discern between performance in a role and being genuine?*
+ *What do you sacrifice in your life for efficiency? When is inefficiency ineffective?*
+ *How do you know that you are in impressing mode?*
+ *What supports you in connecting with your emotions?*
+ *How might stillness be a gateway to loving more fully?*

Our practices are ways of saying "yes" to our journey to our Essence.

Engagement to Counter the Type's Patterns

+ Where in your body do you feel grounded in yourself and safe in who you are? Use this sense of steadiness and stability as a resource when you feel you are shifting into performance mode.
+ Select a project to participate in where you commit to the process rather than the goal and focus on your relationships with the people involved. How does this differ from being goal-focused?
+ Consider who you most want to impress, and why. How would your behavior or demeanor shift if you didn't need to impress? How do you discern between impressing or performing and your genuine self?
+ From your heart space, consider *"Who am I when I'm not producing or accomplishing?"* Journal with this question.

- What tells you that you are shifting from engaging to over-engaging?
- Once a week, take the long way home from work, taking time to notice your surroundings. Practice being inefficient that day.

Often, Threes' beautiful *being* takes a back seat to getting tasks done. Creating space for solitude and stillness invites the fullness of heart. In their heart space, Threes relax into non-doing without fear, for there is no fear in the heart. Beyond roles and image lies Three's radiance.

BEYOND YOUR TYPE

The love you desire from others is discovered in unimpressive acts when your being emerges and doing recedes.

Sabbath-Keeping

Sabbath, in the traditional Jewish understanding, directs our focus to awe and provides space for us to cultivate delight in creation and our lives. Sabbath invites us to wake up to ourselves and our world.

This day's structure is created to slow down the pace of Threes and make space for any emotions that have been suppressed by the week's work. There is no need to be efficient today; no producing or performing is required. Make efforts to forgo your "list of tasks" on Sabbath so your attention can be more directed to your being. By moving slowly, speaking slowly, and eliminating tasks, you heighten your ability to engage your heart. Feelings may arise when you invite them into your awareness to linger a while. Have a practice of uninterrupted stillness—meditation or prayer—that you engage in for at least 20 minutes each Sabbath. When the 20 minutes is up, stay for another three minutes, grounding yourself in order to carry the effects of stillness with you so you can add presence to the doing that follows.

As much as possible, create alone time (or time with an intimate who loves your being). Be with yourself and ask: *What do I enjoy doing just for me? What does my heart want?* You may find yourself engaging in a hobby, reading poetry, gardening, or watching a movie. The key is to relax into your body and be present to yourself rather than outwardly focused. Take care not to make Sabbath an item on a to-do list. If, as you begin this practice, a full day is more than you are able to withstand, begin with half-day Sabbaths and work up to a full day. Be gentle with yourself as you saunter through this day. Saunter to allow your soul time to catch up with you.

A Type Three Prayer

May I create a refuge within for relaxing into my authenticity, a genuineness that dissolves my pretenses. I honor my desire to remove the masks and facades that blind me to who I am, that keep me deceiving myself and others. Ground of Being, guide me deep, slow me down, open my heart, so that the great love within me flows naturally with no need to impress or accomplish. Teach me to honor my fear and doubt, to remember the hesitant one within me that I push aside to continue the performing. Remind me to allow this hesitant one to have a voice in my life, that I may receive wisdom. As I journey to my heart and honor my feelings—my sadness, my anger, my delight—may they encourage me to accept my lovability. I offer gratitude for those in my life who see the real me and love me beyond my doing. May I grow more fully into my Beingness.

CHAPTER 8

The Power of Receiving: Type Two

To some extent, we all seek approval, sometimes without being conscious of it. For Twos, seeking approval is driven by a feeling of being unworthy. Yet, worth is never on the table for any of us. Worthiness is our birthright. What tells you that you have worth? Seated in our own worth, we are steady in ourselves without any need to alter ourselves to fit in. We're already "in." As you read this chapter, invite thoughtfulness from the type Two within you.

> ## TYPE TWO AT A GLANCE
>
> **Strengths:** Good people reader, sees potential in others, enthusiastic
> **Ego Ideal:** I am connected and helpful.
> **Focus of Attention:** Others' needs
> **Motivation:** To receive approval and be affirmed
> **Worldview:** The world is full of interpersonal needs.
> **Fixation:** Flattery
> **Vice:** Pride
> **Holy Idea:** Holy Freedom
> **Virtue:** Humility (balance)

Brief Overview

Twos offer enthusiasm, a positive approach, and a welcoming posture. They are at ease with others and are socially graceful. Twos have a sensitive attunement to people and excel at reading others. Networking comes naturally for them because "connecting" is their specialty. The ability to assess others' gifts and growing edges, then position them where they are most useful, is a Two's gift in organizations. They are good listeners and model an openhearted generosity with grace. When living on automatic, Twos offer help to get approval and affirmation from people they value. The approval of others feels like a lifeline, and when following the automatic patterns of their type, Twos live their lives in such a way as to avoid non-approval and rejection. However, when present with no agenda, Twos are supportive, kind, and fun, reminding us of our best selves.

Two is a rejection-sensitive type, and therefore much effort goes into entering into and remaining in the good graces of others. Focusing on others' needs and attending to them is the Two's strategy for being affirmed. This focus on others directs Twos' energy into over-engaging, over-giving, and over-extending to get approval. Highly sensitive to others they value, Twos notice their likes, dislikes, and strengths. This information is sometimes woven into conversations in the form of flattery, which is the Two's fixation. Winning others over through their sensitive attunement, especially those "tough nuts to crack," is juicy for this type. In terms of connecting, Twos are up to the challenge and can be highly seductive.

Efforts to connect and be affirmed lead to over-giving. If this over-engaging continues, it creates high expectations in others—expectations that Twos will continue in the same mode. Not wanting to disappoint, Twos find themselves living for and attending to others while their own lives shrivel. Eventually, resentment arises. An underlying belief for Twos is that time for the self is available only after taking care of others. This is a false notion, as constant attention to the other leads them to suppress their own desires and needs.

Several years ago, when leading Enneagram panels at our local independent bookstore, I asked the Two panel this question: "All of us like to give and have a need to give. Why do you lead with Two and we don't?" Without missing a beat, one panelist replied, "Because I have to." And that's how it feels within the Two structure. Not helping doesn't seem to be an option. A good inquiry for Twos is, *"Who are you when you aren't helping and no one needs you?"*

The vice of pride keeps Twos working to be indispensable, to be a "saint" in the eyes of others. Pride is in the driver's seat when a Two's internal dialogue is "you need me." Most Twos have a packed schedule. A full calendar gives a sense of connectedness, of being needed and wanted. Twos tend to be defined by others and can lose themselves without the other. Pride may show up as a dismissing of their own suffering.

Solitude, though difficult for this type, is good medicine as it helps Twos return to themselves, consider their own needs, and practice self-care. For those who love Twos, asking them questions about themselves, giving them gentle reminders to attend to themselves, and surprising them with gifts of self-care are **compassionate entry points** that support them in pausing and returning to themselves.

An aspect of pride that sometimes goes unnoticed is the desire to be well-informed. In organizations and groups Twos place themselves in positions of being sought out as listeners, especially when trouble arises. Knowing the inside stories of people can support a feeling of being indispensable and powerful. This information can be strategically used to problem-solve on behalf of the team or sometimes shared with directors or bosses, as Twos seek to be valued. It feels affirming when bosses rely on Twos. Being needed can be an unconscious endgame for this type.

The Striving and the Avoidance

When relationships have strong connections and Twos have avenues of usefulness, life is good. However, this isn't a static moment. Striving to maintain the high regard of others leads them to fill their calendars with supportive endeavors, constantly looking for opportunities to connect and network and devoting attention to requests from others who have come to rely on their support. Setting boundaries is a rare act when the striving to be liked and useful is unconscious. Over time, Twos can become a bit intrusive in their helping. Engaging shifts to over-engaging.

If you lead with Two, what are your body's cues that you are beginning to over-engage? Notice when the thought arises that "you need me." This is a projection that keeps Twos moving toward others and rejecting themselves. A helpful discernment in this moment is to pause and ask yourself, *"Am I helping because I have a need to help, or has the other asked for my help?"* This question may be useful in easing the striving.

A fear of rejection drives over-extending, and it can seem there is plenty of time and energy to help. The old adage "It is better to give than receive" seems to be the mantra for this type. And this little saying has created a crowd of tired Twos—especially female Twos! Isn't it time to name this statement as harmful? Consistently putting ourselves last in line, no matter our type, isn't healthy, nor is it useful to anyone. Yet, our ego structure bombards us with messages crafted to keep our familiar self and habits in motion. Continuing in lockstep with the pattern of constant connecting and giving, can lead to self-rejection. The fear of being rejected is birthed in our own minds much of the time. When we anticipate being rejected, we can see rejection where it doesn't exist.

The defense mechanism for Twos is repression. This operates by blurring feelings and needs and pushing them into the background. Repression is a barrier to self-care and sustains pride in focusing on others' needs. However, to be human is to have needs. Having a need does not equate to neediness (as the Two's ego would have them believe). For Twos, neediness is to be avoided. Noticing the moments when this falsehood arises, naming it as false, and breathing through it brings more internal spaciousness. In this space, it may be possible for Twos to disclose their need and receive support.

When Twos don't have access to their own needs, noticing what they are giving may be a clue to what they themselves desire. When our beloved Twos seem fatigued and aren't expressing their needs, a **compassionate entry point** is to offer an act of service on their behalf without asking them what they need.

The Core Fear and the Pivot

Feeling useless and unneeded can feel like death to people who lead with type Two. A key illusion is that worth and lovability are dependent on being connected and useful. Foundational work for Twos is to learn to separate love from helping, usefulness, or approval. Unearned love is difficult to understand or receive if worth hinges on being needed. If you lead with Two, observe your body and your heart's response when someone offers you love unexpectedly. Do you deflect? Minimize? What would support you in receiving?

We all know the joy in giving to others without anticipating anything in return. Why deny others that joy? In Narrative Enneagram Intensives, Dr. Daniels often shared this wisdom: "If I can only give to you and not receive, then my giving is a form of taking because I expect something in return. When giving is genuine, it is the same act as receiving." It isn't a transaction. Giving and receiving are in the same flow when they come from the same source—the heart. Receiving enriches relationships. *Receiving is an act of hospitality* and plays a role in how we care for and relate to those we love. This balance facilitates mutuality in relating.

Twos: *Your generous and hospitable heart is nurtured by the gifts and support of others.*

Companion Voices

As you read the stories from the companion writers, be open to finding a part of you in their shared experiences.

Finding balance in work or career is tricky for Twos. **Iyabo**, our next contributor, speaks to the challenge of being the power behind the throne and her path of return to herself.

I put the phone on the counter and held myself up by leaning on the sink. I tilted my head slightly backward to beckon the tears back from whence they came. I did not want to cry. I was too tired.

Finally, I took several deep breaths. I made my coffee and then, in a few minutes, I found myself feeling lighter and not so teary-eyed. "What happened?" I asked myself. Bemused, I became aware of good feelings. I observed that the pit of my stomach was calm and that the familiar lump in my throat was not there. I noticed that I did not have an urge to call someone to avoid feeling my feelings. The desire to cry and the bone-weariness in my body soon gave way to a smile and a chuckle.

I allowed the goodness in and finally figured it out. The previous night, I had facilitated a challenging workshop which had left me psychologically exhausted. I was spent. I also had not slept well. I woke up to a racing brain, and my emotions felt as if they were dancing on my skin, living outside of me, and creating great discomfort. They were trying to get my attention.

I had just called my work partner at Compassionate Atlanta to process the previous evening with her, but she was busy and had been short with me before scurrying off. Immediately, this short conversation brought up powerful emotions of rejection and desolation—I felt so unworthy and alone in this world. I felt deeply rejected by the rushed tone of her voice as she told me about her busyness. Hence, the attempted tears.

"Hello, old friend. I know you," I said, smiling at the recognition of the unhealthy engraved pattern of leading from Enneagram type Two. "Wow, that is so cool. I recognize you and I am not even mad. I don't get to squash you down. Okay. Stay there. Iyabo, what do you need now?"

I gave myself a couple of hours to be quiet and sit with the awareness of what I was feeling. Later, I texted my work partner and asked for a call back. I told her that I needed to debrief and wanted emotional support as the workshop had left me depleted. She called, and we had a great conversation. It helped me banish the lingering vestiges of insecurity and rejection. Soon, I felt restored and whole again.

Shocked at the ease of naming what I wanted and asking for it, I said, "Self, who is this and what have you done with Iyabo?" As weary as my body felt and as much as I just craved the nothingness of binge-watching mindless TV, I was impressed with my ability to take care of myself and not wallow in rejection as I used to do.

I came from Africa to the United States at age 16, away from home and parents, to get an education and create a life for myself. Forty-plus years later, as a single, childless, Black woman who has always tied my dignity to my production, I have only recently been able to disengage work from the sum of my self-worth. I once started a business and felt an increased positive self-image, but that soon faded. I hated the isolation of overseeing an organization and making hard decisions alone. I loathed that the buck stopped with me. Fifteen years later, I closed the business.

After a particularly challenging period in my life, including the failure of that business, I moved into a "power behind the throne" position. I took a job out of emotional, psychological, and financial desperation. It felt like heaven. Generosity and openness characterized this job, and I had the opportunity to grow and develop new skills.

With no more responsibility for everything and everyone, I focused on just one person, and I loved every aspect of it. I took great pride in being the "favorite" worker. I enjoyed being depended upon and delivering on what I said I would do. I delighted in knowing the thinking patterns of this person and anticipating their next moves and needs without being asked. I loved being the confidante. I relaxed into the constant interaction and access to this person's entire life. I felt affirmed by the business trips as well as the side trips to find expensive presents for their spouse. I especially loved being the gatekeeper and protecting my boss's availability. I found my worth in being overly focused on this person and all the accompanying minutiae that show up in my work.

I enjoyed it all.

Until I didn't.

It started with irregular paychecks, which disrupted my finances. When I asked for what I needed, my requests were not well received, and yet I smiled and pretended all was well. I ignored the red flags, including late-night phone calls to finish up work-related items, and the violation of my schedule and my priorities. I extended myself beyond my job description and observed no boundaries with time management. I also ignored the fact that I was underemployed and overqualified for this job.

Finally, another person came into the picture and became the favorite. Suddenly, my access to my boss shrank. The foundation of my worthiness was taken away. No more confidences, no more organizing, no more opinions sought or given. My calls were no longer answered. I felt hurt and abandoned. My blood raged with the pain of rejection and my body ached with self-loathing.

I labeled my first interpretation of the change in the relationship status as "rejection." This was proof positive that I was unlovable and a constant screw-up. Once again, this was universal evidence that my needs were irrelevant and harmful and that their mere articulation resulted in mayhem in my life. I became depressed, felt worthless, and considered myself a failure at everything. I could neither run a business nor keep a job, and that meant certain poverty, homelessness, or even death for me.

My support system convinced me to discover the power within me to change my work narrative. I could not afford to have an unstable work life, and I wanted work to be joyful. I chose not to run away from that pain while exploring what had gone wrong. I took responsibility for my part and made changes. I owned my role in the mishap.

A wise African American elder once told me, "In every dime are two nickels. Make sure you know your nickel." In conflict, no side is ever 100% right or wrong. To truly resolve a conflict, we must take responsibility for our part. I had to own my own nickel in this dime. I ruthlessly told myself the truth. I refused to judge myself, coddle the hurt, diminish my self-worth, or blame myself. I discovered a mixed bag of wonderful experiences as well as some bad ones.

Armed with a brand-new journal and commitment to self-awareness, I began my research project to evaluate what I could change. I reviewed my calendar, delved into my computer for old documents and timelines, and created a chronology. I noticed that my very first paycheck was not delivered on time, and I did not say anything. I observed that I never stated my needs and did not invite reciprocity into the relationship. I counted my contributions to the organization and wrote out the many genuine benefits of the job as well. I owned my nickel in this dime.

For a couple of weeks, I discussed what came up with those closest to me *ad nauseum*. I concluded that this could have been the perfect job if I had not allowed my unrecognized and unarticulated "need to be liked" to mar the relationship. I dug deeper into the Enneagram. I leaned into my type Four resource point to remember who I was and focus on my creative strengths. I also tapped into my type One wing and made the decision to conduct work relationships the "right" way.

After multiple jobs, I now balance my own independent consulting with gratifying social justice work at Compassionate Atlanta, where my work partner and I share power as co-directors. This means openness, care, and mutuality in our work relationship. I embrace that I do not have to be the power on the throne, or the power behind the throne. There is no throne anymore. There is just a circle where we are interdependent and share power to support a better and more compassionate world.

"No throne" indicates that no one has more worth than others. The beautiful unfolding of Iyabo's career demonstrates the work of inquiry into type patterns and the removal blinders for the sake of balance and mutuality. She checked facts, named her missteps, and made changes. Intentionally engaging in inner and outer work together is powerful, painful, and life-giving.

Our next contributor, **Chelsea**, shares her experience of, ultimately, belonging to herself. Separating being needed from being loved, she discovers that she is useful and powerful "when I prioritize addressing what I need and pour from an already full cup." Paradoxically, self-care is the foundation for supporting others.

It was the fall of 2013 when I first encountered the Enneagram as a resource for my own becoming. I had previously heard whisperings about it, but I didn't know much more than "there are nine numbers that people say can tell you a lot about yourself." However, that fall, as a student at Wake Forest Divinity School, I sat in Chris Copeland's class "Spirituality and the Enneagram" and I saw myself in full view for what felt like the first time. In that moment, I heard what was happening within me spoken loudly in clear and well-articulated prose. At the same time, while folks were guessing each other's numbers, many of my friends decided that I was an Enneagram Three. I laughed alongside them, knowing my behavior confirmed their opinion when in truth, I knew without a doubt that I lead with type Two, the Helper or Giver. I knew because that type's vice is pride, and the thought of admitting I actually had needs that needed to be addressed stressed me all the way out.

Reading this sentence confirmed my knowing that I lead with Two: "Twos often need to be needed and can feel a sense of pride about being everything to everyone." I knew that my goals, accolades, and sense of accomplishment were all rooted in what I felt like the world needed from me. If I was great, I was helping my parents feel proud and confident in who I was in the world. If I had the highest levels of education from great schools, I could get a good job and be the friend who could give everyone whatever they wanted. If I was a minister, I literally helped people for a living. If I did <you fill in the blank>, I could fulfill a need around me and never have to admit that often I was not addressing my own needs.

Reading the description of type Two didn't feel great at first. It felt like someone had thrust me in front of a mirror I had been avoiding. I felt seen in a way that felt like home, and also almost *too* seen, in a way that felt invasive. In front of that mirror, I realized I was outsourcing all my energy, directing it everywhere but at myself. Everyone was getting the best of me except for me.

Everyone else was encountering this encouraging, gregarious, excited, and focused human, but to myself I was critical, rude, and also not fully present to the truths of my own story. Even when people asked me if I needed help, I would often deflect and say no, while offering it to them. It was almost as if I was keeping track in my mind so that I was always the burden carrier and never the burden. Pride has many faces and forms. For me, it looked like "I can be everything, and in turn, I need nothing."

The gift of the Enneagram was learning that, while I enjoyed being helpful and important in the lives of those around me and the systems I partake in, I couldn't be great if I wasn't willing to be well and offer myself my own love. I learned that wellness isn't about being needed by others, it is about affirming that I am always a being that needs me. Through this exploration I developed my mantra, "I need me first, and I need me most." To some this might sound selfish, but for me it's a signal to check in with my activities and ask: Am I working to fill a need or desire at the cost of my own wellness? Am I fulfilling needs around me without addressing the ones that are within me? I ask these questions every day.

My impulse to be everything to everybody has lessened through a lot of work and good therapy. However, this compulsion is still present, and sometimes I can feel like I am not doing enough when I center my own wellness. But in truth, I am my best self to the ecosystem of my communities and this world at large when I prioritize addressing what I need and pour from an already full cup. In that same vein, the more I make sure my cup is full, the more I realize the amazing relationships I have, which pour into me without my knowing it. I learned that when I am available to love and can receive it, love doesn't come fragmented, but in full from myself and the community that surrounds me in love.

Reflecting on this type Two self, I realize that so many of these patterns have been affirmed from childhood. I grew up knowing that if I could keep everyone happy there would be more peace in the space, and I would also feel a sense of accomplishment from filling the needs I perceived. For better and for worse, I was the friend anyone could go to, and I would do anything for anybody. I also can get manipulative when I feel unneeded. I can start creating avenues to help, where honestly, my help just isn't what's required. With an uncritical mind, going beyond the call of duty sounds like a beautiful thing. Indeed, it is, until you are not one of the things you go above and beyond for.

As a Black woman in the United States, I live in a society that assumes that I should labor. I live in a societal framework that asks me to work for a sense of worthiness, without taking any accountability for the historical frameworks that have violently created a caricature of incessant neediness of the world Black women are supposed to fulfill. Black women have been mothers to their children as well as the children of their slave masters, whose violence toward them was constant. Black women have been asked to see themselves as labor and not life. So, being a Black woman motivated to fulfill the needs of all those around her, often to the detriment of my own flourishing, fit right into a white supremacist model of who I was "supposed" to be. Few people asked questions as I burned out, saying "yes" to others and "no" to my own wellness and well being. It was and is my daily choice to choose to see myself beyond any caricature and to know that to be loved doesn't mean to be needed. More importantly, I need me and I love me first.

I used to think to be needed was to belong. I thought that to be needed was to be loved, and so much around me confirmed that. I felt deeply that to be needed was to be worthy. To be needed was to exist, because without it, who was I?

Now I know to be is to be worthy of all the love that I can receive, and from that place of abundance I can give freely and fully without guilt or abandon—first to myself and then to all those whom I have the gift of encountering. I know in the depths of my heart that I am worth the time it takes to know me, the practices it takes to care for me, and the gift of simply being in my own presence as a mandatory place of renewal and self-love. I am able to be loved by others much better now because I let myself articulate what I need and what I want. I have learned that so many people just didn't know that I was available to receive. This journey is not always easy, but it's one that I am grateful to be on. I love that my orientation is to be helpful, to help those around me belong, and to offer the best of myself in any situation. I love even more that I am now a part of the ecosystem of my own care. As I say to my mirror each morning, *I need me first, and I need me most.*

Chelsea offers a great insight that Twos live in the illusion that "to be needed is to belong." And she concludes with powerful wisdom for all of us: Self-love isn't selfish. It is kindness.

Alchemy: From Type to Essence

Holy Freedom as Enlightened Spiritual Perspective

The avoidance of being useless and the striving to be connected and needed set Twos up for a life filled with others' expectations of them. Eventually, Twos sense their desire for their own lives. The first step on the path to freedom from the expectations of others is setting boundaries. Twos' virtue of humility brings balance as it allows Twos to be realistic about their own expectations. With this clarity, a "no" is spoken as easily as a "yes." Humility brings groundedness and sets the stage for receptivity. Hidden agendas and control dissolve in a receptive posture. Willful becomes willing, and Twos move in a natural flow of events, comfortable with a holy unfolding. The Two's categories of "dispensable" and "indispensable" do not exist when they live in the knowing that are all are valued and loved equally for our Beingness, Twos included.

As Twos come to know themselves as lovable and worthy, the need for others' approval vanishes. In Holy Freedom, Twos are free to attend to their own needs, to set boundaries, to practice self-care, and to receive love without earning it. Standing in the truth of who they are—knowing their strengths and limitations—the "yes" becomes a true "yes" because, without need of approval, Twos can voice their "no." Helping arises from the heart, a heart no longer held captive by pride. Released from approval ratings, Twos become teachers in genuine helping *and* in gracious receiving. A natural flow emerges.

PRACTICES Bringing Awareness to Two's Core Issues

Focused Inquiry

+ *When is helping a barrier to your loving fully?*

+ *Who would you be if no one needed you? Who are you when you aren't connecting and helping?*

+ *What is your particular brand of approval-seeking? How do you alter yourself when seeking approval?*

+ *How do you use helping to control? How might receiving enable you to love more fully?*

+ *In what ways are you receptive? What is your felt sense of receptivity?*

Our practices are ways of saying "yes" to our journey to our Essence.

Engagement to Counter the Type's Patterns

+ At least twice each week, ask someone for help with a project or personal need. Notice the feelings that come up. Allow and feel the feelings until they dissipate.

+ Practice receiving with an open heart and without reciprocating. Simply receive and take into your body that you are worthy.

+ When you start to move to help or assist someone, remain still for 10 seconds. Breathe through any unease. Observe what arises within yourself and in the external situation.

+ What body cues tell you that you are seeking approval? Pause for a few seconds before engaging.

+ Notice when you are using flattery excessively, and with whom. Inquire into what is driving this.

Twos are so attuned to others' needs that they may assume those of us leading with other types have this sensitivity as well, that we should be able to intuit the Two's needs. We can't. Naming your needs and wants is crucial for Twos, as we non-Twos are often more clueless!

BEYOND YOUR TYPE

Your willingness to receive from others and to name what you need, supports the process of self-acceptance and claiming your worth.

Sabbath-Keeping

Sabbath, in the traditional Jewish understanding, directs our focus to awe and provides space for us to cultivate delight in creation and our lives. Sabbath invites us to wake up to ourselves and our world.

This day's rhythm is designed to create a sense of freedom for Twos, who can easily use all of their time on behalf of others. As much as you can, use this Sabbath to "help yourself" to whatever you needed during the week that you repressed. You may want to make a list of your needs and be willing to experience these needs (knowing we all have needs) as guides to reconnect with yourself. On this day, disconnect from those whose approval you most seek. When your mind's focus goes to the lives of others and what they want or need, planning to connect or help, simply redirect your attention to your own needs. Take care that your energy stays with you, rather than using it to telephone or email others.

Each Sabbath, ask others to do something for you. This may be simply to enjoy a fun activity together or to give you time to yourself. (If you're a grandparent, this is not a day to take care of the grandchildren!) Create a sacred space where you can read, meditate, and be still for at least 20 minutes as a part of your Sabbath. Reflect on your own limitations and remind yourself of these as a protection from over-extending. Then, reflect on your own inherent goodness. Consider how it guides your living and decision making. Ask yourself, *"How did I approve of myself this past week?"*

A Type Two Prayer

As I greet each day, may I anchor myself in humility, honoring my gifts as well as my limitations. I desire to be real. I desire to be discerning in what is mine to do and not to do. Ground of Being, empty me of my need for approval and my belief in all who need me. Guide me in the ways of being receptive, that I may participate more fully in my own life, offering myself compassion as well as others. May I be more available to my own needs and to the present unfolding without agendas as my pride dissolves. Open my heart to the support of others. Remind me of my interdependence so that I no longer inflate my own abilities, but am grounded in the reality of who I am. Grant me a willingness to be open to what arises, that I may find my freedom in choosing myself.

CHAPTER 9

The Power of Belonging: Type Four

Throughout our lives, we all experience times of emotional depth, whether despair, grief, or joy. For those who lead with type Four, emotions feel like home, not a place to visit from time to time. Emotional depth feels authentic to this type, and in fact it is authentic when this "depth" isn't co-opted by the Four's ego ideal, "I am unique." Authenticity need not have trumpets sounding to be real. It can appear in the most ordinary of moments and in small acts. What tells you you're being authentic? Consider this as you read this chapter, listening with the type Four within.

TYPE FOUR AT A GLANCE

Strengths: Emotionally intuitive, creative, keen aesthetic
Ego Ideal: I am unique, different.
Focus of Attention: What is missing
Motivation: To long for what was or could be
Worldview: The world is an abandoning place.
Fixation: Melancholy
Vice: Envy
Holy Idea: Holy Source
Virtue: Equanimity

Brief Overview

Fours have a strong desire to find meaning in their lives and work. They appreciate beauty, creativity, and innovative thinking and are drawn to high ideals. They are seekers, open to learning and new thinking. Their inner lives are rich. People leading with this type are comfortable with sadness and emotional pain. They can easily be with others who are experiencing difficult times without trying to "fix it." They are gifted at dealing with situations that are outside the ordinary. Fours can name the elephant in the room if it needs naming and aren't fearful of intensity. In fact, Fours may perceive intensity as bringing a realness to the moment, so they can become intense when situations or relationships get too comfortable. And when others engage with intensity, Fours can shift into a calm presence, since others are supplying the intensity.

With a focus of attention on what is missing, the Four's energy goes into seeking, searching, and longing—this type's motivation. It's worthy to note that longing denies Fours their authenticity, because they aren't in the present moment. When Fours feel that authentic connection is missing, they lean into being unique or different, believing this facilitates a deeper connection. While this can be true, the drive to be unique may also serve to disconnect Fours from others, as in their uniqueness they may seek out peak experiences and disregard ordinary times, the moments between the peaks. Strong relationships can be birthed and deepened in the simple times when we remember that as humans, we are more alike than different. Questions for consideration for Fours include *"Who would you be if nothing were missing?"* and *"How does being unique or different disconnect you from others?"*

Envy is the emotional habit or vice of this type, and when envy is in control, Fours engage in comparisons. With an internal ideal of "how I should be" (or how others should be), Fours can reject what is real in favor of the ideal. The grass is greener anywhere but in the now. If the comparison relates to the self, then feelings of inadequacy or shame may arise. Self-rejection can follow on the heels of inner narratives whispering "I'm too much" or "I'm not enough." In these false narratives, Fours remain ungrounded and unsatisfied. "(I Can't Get No) Satisfaction" is the theme song of the moment, and disappointment is playing lead guitar. Comparison robs us of our joy. Good medicine in these moments is to move into gratefulness for something or someone. Gratefulness and a comparing mind can't coexist. My astute type Four friend Ronda tells me she's realizing that "Joy can exist alongside and in the midst of the missing and incomplete." This is a rich learning and a beautiful expansion.

Those who lead with Four are at home in emotions and can be absorbed by them. They easily attune to and take in the emotions of others, but they may then become unaware of which emotions are their own and which belong to others. Setting boundaries is essential. Many Fours continue to carry the emotions of their family of origin long into adulthood. A ritual of letting go can be helpful in discerning between their own emotions and those of others, allowing the latter to be gently released. Recently I sat with a Four friend on an evening marked by a new moon. By firelight, she named the emotions she had carried that were not hers and that she was ready to surrender. After writing each one down on a piece of paper, she offered it to the fire. The paper turning to ash and rising into the air facilitated a beautiful clearing for her. Then, gratefulness emerged.

At times, emotions can rule the day for Fours when moods are left unexplored. Remembering that "feelings aren't reality" supports a return to the facts of a situation, especially when Fours take comments or circumstances personally. Taking personally something that isn't personal is a form of suffering, and Fours can become overly engaged with inner stories that create a sense of melancholy. When this occurs, consider the facts. Allow facts to lead rather than feelings:

lead with facts while honoring emotions that arise. A question that I pose to Fours who are in this state is, "Who are you aside from your melancholy?" Pulling wisdom from Internal Family Systems work, we learn that only a part of us is sad. For those who love Fours, a **compassionate entry point** can be asking simple questions that return them to the facts of reality.

Sometimes, I'll recommend to type Four clients who are caught in the self-sabotaging trap of personalizing and have abandoned themselves to emotions that they *connect with their inner elder* and seek wisdom from this part of themselves. The inner elder brings a balance and can restore sanity through the varying waves of intense emotion. A key discernment for this type is noticing when they attempt to create depth through intense emotion rather than allowing depth to arise organically.

Creative expression is a gift of this type, and many Fours report that engaging in creativity can sink them into the present moment, moving them out of comparisons. When present, Fours can relax into their wholeness, deeply connect with themselves, and see the extraordinary in all.

The Striving and the Avoidance

The Four's striving is for peak experiences. The emotional intensity of peak experiences glistens with the aura of authenticity and depth, and Fours feel at home here. A sense of belonging occurs in the highs of these intense encounters. If not immersed in the peaks of life, then Fours can linger in the valleys as well. Life between peaks and valleys can be difficult, because it seems too ordinary. Fours see the ordinary as a place of disconnection, so they avoid it. The mundane and the practical can seem boring, yet life is lived in the "in between" times, and the work for Fours is to find ease in this middle ground. To encourage themselves in this endeavor, Fours might consider, *"What depth does the ordinary offer?"*

Peak experiences feed into the Four's ego ideal, "I am unique, different." Being unique takes many forms and is itself a comparison. Unique from whom? Different from what? As a Four once shared with me, "If I strive to be successful and I am a success, it won't measure up to my inner ideal of what success 'should be.' I'll be disappointed. So, I prefer to be unique." Fours often report that longing for something is more appealing than attaining it.

Longing arises from the defense mechanism for Fours: introjection. Simply put, this means comparing reality to one's inner ideal. This could be the ideal self, ideal lover, ideal work. Regardless, reality rarely measures up. Disappointment is familiar to Fours, and it spawns the mental fixation of melancholy, which in turn drives longing. When longing takes hold, self-aware Fours can use this as a means to nudge themselves forward, to take steps toward that which they long for rather than allowing melancholy to rule. This is a choice point for Fours. When our beloved Fours are in this melancholy state, offering an abiding presence rather than giving advice or trying to fix them is a **compassionate entry point.** The ability to "be with" is itself a balm for this type. Engaging in practical tasks can be a lifeline in melancholy moments: cook food, wash clothes, chop wood.

The Core Fear and the Pivot

The worldview of Fours is that the world is an abandoning place. Abandonment is a core fear. This fear, propped up by feelings of deficiency, leads Fours to be sensitive to disconnection and the notion that "I don't belong." When the fear of abandonment is strong, Fours are blind to supportive connections. As this fear surfaces into consciousness, an appropriate inquiry is the question, *"How do I abandon myself?"* This can generate key insights that serve to alert Fours to moments of leaving themselves. Self-abandonment follows on the heels of envy's comparisons and engenders moods of melancholy. Asking *"What do I appreciate about myself?"* may be useful during these times, along with setting a time limit on how long to linger in this mood and storyline. Belonging begins with self. A **compassionate entry point** for those who love Fours is to remind them of our support of them and of our appreciation of their support of us.

The natural world is a great teacher in grounding, belonging, and authenticity. No roles or performance are needed. The land holds us, does not abandon us, and returns us to ourselves. The great Oak teaches us steadiness. The potential of "extraordinary" lies in the ordinary small seed or acorn of the Oak tree. Authenticity isn't necessarily dramatic or big or bold. Nothing is more real than a handful of seeds that become nourishing food months later or beautiful life-giving trees years later. Working with seeds and the land is a good reminder that steadiness in the ordinary renders beautiful results.

When grounded in presence, Fours return to themselves and know they are enough. Gratefulness abounds as longing shifts to belonging in the present moment. The virtue of equanimity arises in this grounded state, bringing a mental and emotional evenness. As steadiness and simple engagement take the lead, Fours cease magnifying perceptions. Inner calm and a compassionate heart arise.

Fours: *Simple sadness and simple joy expand the heart, allowing you to feel a deep calm and connection with the other.*

Companion Voices

As you read the stories from the companion writers, be open to finding a part of you in their shared experiences.

In this narrative, **Dorrie** shares some of her experiences of the Four structure, demonstrating how the shift from longing to appreciating dissolves the comparing mind. Her keen inner observer returns her to the present, where suffering ceases.

> While accompanying my mother on a doctor's visit in another city recently, my thoughts wandered to how it would feel to live in the apartments or condos I saw outside the window. They looked new, colorful, and like a cool place to live. I thought about the new development they were in and imagined how convenient it must feel to live in an area that includes retail shops within walking distance. I imagined that all of the amenities there were better than where I live. I was disregarding how much I love my home, my humongous yard, and all of my bird friends who visit my trees, feeders, and baths. I wasn't thinking about how much I love living in metro Atlanta. And I certainly wasn't thinking that I have zero desire to move to South Carolina. I was disregarding the goodness of my life and escaping the moment of facing my mother's declining health.
>
> I'm certain that I have had millions of similar longings, triggered by a need to escape the moment. I've spent my entire life wanting to do something else, wanting to live somewhere else, wanting to find my very special purpose. At times, I also looked longingly at others' seemingly ideal lives. After numerous doctor's visits with my mother, I started thinking that being a doctor was a great job where you get to solve a puzzle of sorts, determining the root of someone's distress, then you get to help them feel better! I wondered why I didn't consider medical school years ago. In hindsight, I was being envious of doctors' lives and

idealizing them. In reality, I had disconnected from the privilege and pleasure of being able to care for my ailing mother.

Escaping the moment sometimes shifts me into an imagined future. This was certainly true in the past, when I let envy and idealization impact my romantic relationships. I did not let a Sunday go by without reading about weddings in the *New York Times*. I couldn't wait to see how people met, fell in love, and celebrated it all at their wedding. I envied the people in those stories and longed to experience the same kind of love. I wanted to find an ideal partner and live happily ever after. For many of those years, this longing wasn't even possible because same-gender marriage was illegal. It also wasn't possible because I had idealized strangers' relationships so much that I was rarely fully present enough to participate in my own relationships or to figure out if I was actually compatible with whomever I was dating at the time. Instead, I was busy trying to make the fantasy fit.

With little connection to myself or the need I was trying to fill, I discovered that many of my relationships were not sustainable once I tuned into reality. (I hope my past girlfriends will accept this blanket apology.) There were many fantastic times and experiences, and I am grateful for the lessons I learned on the path to my authentic self and the present moment. With therapy and lessons learned, I am a lot more grounded and able to fully enjoy the moments of my wonderful relationship with an amazing woman. Marriage is not a priority now that I can enjoy my relationship for how it enhances rather than defines my life.

Longing and envy affected other areas of my life, too. And they gave me a persistent feeling that something was missing. For the majority of a 30-year journalism career, which I largely enjoyed, I felt something was missing. I felt as if I was missing the mark on living out my purpose. I would often ask people questions about their work and think that if I could do what they did, I would be happy. It wasn't too long before

I realized that I was doing it again, continuing a pattern of longing rather than action. I entered therapy again, this time with the aid of the Enneagram, which helped move me out of my head and into self-awareness and the recognition of my own agency. This new perspective led me to leave journalism and enroll in Candler School of Theology at Emory University, where I earned a Master of Divinity degree.

Discovering the Enneagram was a game changer. As I listened to others who lead with type Four share the inner workings of their minds, I wondered how they knew my thoughts; it was like listening to myself. I was not weird or extremely different. I was not alone in my longings or the trying on of other people's lives. I came to understand how voids in my life affected how I processed the world. I also learned ways to pull myself back into the moment and how to stay grounded. The Enneagram showed me what "success" looked like in terms of overcoming how I clouded and escaped life experiences. I discovered how to shift my attention away from self-focused thoughts so that I could enjoy people, experiences, and beauty in the world.

Birding is one of the experiences that help me to shift away from navel-gazing. When birding, I get lost in the beauty of nature. I think of nothing else but what's before me—flashes of color, familiar songs, the flutter of wings—and trying to capture the perfect photo to help make the moments last longer. When I'm birding, I'm fully present to all the Creator offers; it's not an escape but an openness to the moment. Birding provides a respite from my type Four patterns.

In a similar way of letting the universe act on me, I practice Centering Prayer to still my mind and open myself to Spirit. Centering Prayer is a type of rest I need from myself and the world. It's my time to refuel and silence my thoughts. I am able to open myself to let Spirit guide me so that I can experience life as it unfolds. I wish that I could say that I practice Centering Prayer consistently. Sometimes I have consistent stretches of practice, and other times I feel off-kilter and remember that I need to resituate myself in the world.

I wish that I could say that therapy, the Enneagram, life experiences, birding, Centering Prayer, and the like bring an end to patterns of long-ing, envy, idealization, and noticing what is missing. But they have not, and I hope they never do. As a Black queer woman from the South, my life experience provides a filter that highlights oppression. There's much to long for in this nation and world. I can't stop longing for all of humankind to have the right to live freely and thrive, regardless of how different their being is from white-centered, dominant culture and its trappings. I can't stop noticing how often queer people, Black people, and women are left out of the picture. I can't help noticing how many theologies center on a God defined by the white, dominant culture. I idealize a world in which "do no harm" is how we treat each other. This is really my ideal love story.

I now know it's okay to long for a better world and not necessary to long for a better self. It's a balance I try to hold on to. Living a meaning-ful life does not require me to be extraordinary; it just requires me to be present, offering whatever I can in the moment. And now that I have let go of trying to be extraordinary, I am able to embrace a vocational path inspired by my own life experience that gives me joy while I aim to help others live authentic lives. The path to understand, accept, and love my Black, Queer, and Southern self has been a long and necessary one. And now that I have found comfort with myself, I realize it requires spiritual practice to stay on the path.

Self-acceptance leads us to understand that we belong and always will. There is no need to be different or extraordinary. Equanimity arises in these moments, and spiritual practices strengthen the con-stancy of this knowing, as Dorrie so beautifully expresses.

Cathy, our next contributor, teaches us about how the "control" feature for Fours has shown up in her life, as well as the natural bent toward peak experiences.

After studying and teaching the Enneagram for a quarter century, I know it's an inexhaustible subject, and new insights often surprise me. I recently learned something about the type I lead with, type Four, that had never before sunk in: We like to be in control.

This perspective on type Four is at odds with the conventional view of the romantic, artist, or individualist. Fours are perceived—and often experience ourselves—as flighty, unorganized, scattered, emotional. This is hardly the skill set I would have associated with being in control. But as described below, being "in control" means something very specific in the life of a Four.

When I think of someone as controlling, I think of a person who wants to demand, negotiate, bully, resist, or manipulate another into doing their bidding. But when I think of type Fours and control, that's not it. (Admittedly, type Four drama can be a method of control, intended or not.) I believe that I want everyone to have exactly what they want and am motivated to help them find it. A wise friend I knew answered questions about how many children she had by saying, "I have eight only children." As a type Four, I take great satisfaction in seeing that look of pleasure, of being seen for who you truly are, in someone's— anyone's—eyes. We all give what we want to receive, right?

As a type Four, I am caught in a struggle between presenting my authentic or unique self, while at the same time directing others away from judging the tender self beneath. Committed to authenticity, we Fours fear that our unknown self must be unlovable and is likely to be rejected. Either way, this shaky attempt to strike a balance between authenticity and performance requires a lot of control. So, my issue with control tends to have more to do with managing the other's response toward me than getting them to do or not do something for me. I want to manage their perception of who I am—their evaluation of my value. Managing the other's response toward me arises from my natural emotional sensitivity as a Four.

With this emotional sensitivity, highs and lows are an innate part of my life. In its healthy manifestation, this is joyous engagement with the ebb and flow of experience. But without underlying equanimity—the ability to maintain calm composure even in difficulty—ups and downs become volatile instability instead. During my Enneagram Teacher Certification week, Dr. David Daniels remarked that he had identified a "Junkie" label for all the other types: Harmony Junkie (Nine), Certainty Junkie (Six), Perfection Junkie (One)—you get the idea. But he hadn't figured out type Four. He asked those of us on the Four panel what kind of Junkies Fours might be. Without hesitation I replied, "That's easy. 'Peak Experience' Junkies." "Yes," he acknowledged, "that's it."

Here is a ridiculous, yet accurate, example of my assumptions and search for a peak or exquisite experience. Years ago, a client was on his way to pick me up to attend a business meeting. He had just come from a cocktail reception and asked me to stop and pick up breath mints and a cup of coffee. When I finally got to the car, he asked, "What took you so long?" I smiled and handed him a package of Italian mints and a cappuccino. He laughed and said, "I just meant black coffee and a roll of Life Savers."

It is interesting that, even as a white, cis woman, as a type Four I experience myself as different and therefore an outsider. I like to think we Fours are usually accepting of differences, a characteristic this type values. I am empathetic and readily relate to suffering. But I have also learned to be careful not to make too many assumptions; just because I live with a sense of abandonment does not mean that I understand the experience of those who have been marginalized.

I was in my forties when, thanks to the Enneagram, I finally understood my hesitation to ask a question or make a comment in a class, conference, or meeting unless I was pretty sure no one else would think of it. I finally realized that having to be "one of a kind" creates a performance quality to participation that subsumed my innate curiosity and interest in other people. Besides, it's exhausting.

It's difficult—no, impossible—to maintain a level of energy in which every experience needs to be exquisite. Here is how that plays out. I am hanging out with friends or family. My definition of hanging out is likely to omit the "hanging" aspect. From my teenage years and well into adulthood, my family assigned shifts among themselves to keep up with my activity level. It's not just my desire to be exhilarated. I felt compelled to provide the same experience for the rest of the group, as though anything less was somehow letting everyone down. On that pivot, participation becomes all or nothing. Unless everyone is caught up in the excitement, I can tend to fade into the background.

In this struggle to balance authenticity and social acceptance, I am trained to a posture in which I walk a tightrope in high heels. In short, controlled. The early reactions of, first, family, and later friends and colleagues to emotional sensitivity generally teach me to at least try to tamp down volatility. This effort conflicts with my commitment to be authentic and a desire for a radical honesty that does not always comport with social convention. That is the tightrope.

I am finely tuned to my own emotions, sure, and have to learn that emotions are information, not edicts or license. At the same time, I am exquisitely attuned to the emotions of others. One client referred to this as his "Spidey Sense," this intuitive sense of others' emotional tone.

This sense served me very well during two decades as a trial lawyer. It allowed me to walk into a courtroom—every pore open—attuned to the emotional tone of 15 strangers, if you count 12 jurors, two alternates, and a judge. On the other hand, it has taken me much longer to grasp how a fleeting look across someone's face that leaves me tender and guarded may not even have registered with them.

A good friend, also a type Four, recently told me she has begun saying to friends and family who comment on her sensitivity, "Yes, I am an empath." We resonate with others' emotional energy, and the low rumbling of suffering is especially difficult to ignore. When someone suffers, we suffer along with them, so we are doubly motivated to see that people avoid occasions of suffering. That effort can involve meddling, which doesn't serve us or the others we seek to help.

Still, we try. As a parent, I've seen this tendency at work. Of course, we all want the best for our children, but being acutely empathetic can make it extra challenging to watch while others learn by dealing with their own challenges. I try to remember to assure my children that their decisions from a grounded place tend to be good ones, even if they aren't what someone else (me, for example) might have decided. Stepping back and reminding myself I can't possibly know what is in someone else's best interests is my work.

I imagine if I responded to a survey asking what one change would most improve my life, I might say "lighten up." Recalling that everything about the Enneagram seems to be a paradox, these days I'm trying to remember that lightening up is an antidote to control. That control is a barrier to the workings of Mystery and to the joy that is here right now. That peak experience is a false high. That setting good boundaries is a better path to true connection than over-functioning and trampling around in someone else's business.

While all types have to learn that trying to control emotions is a nonstarter, as a Four, I need to recognize and make peace with them, allowing emotions to move through me while deciphering the lessons they bring. Leading with type Four reminds me of my friend Hannah, an interior designer, whose sense of color is pitch perfect. I have seen her leave a room, pained because the green in a couch cushion is a couple of shades off. Like a Mantis shrimp, she is bombarded by colors I can't perceive. Similarly, it's just that we Fours have such a delicate emotional tuning fork—something I'll probably enjoy more as I learn to lighten up.

Types in the Enneagram's heart triad have a sensitivity to being unlovable. Cathy articulates some of the inner narratives and thought processes that bring this notion of being unlovable forward. Additionally, Cathy offers a great insight by naming the peak experience as a false high that blocks Fours from authentic connection. To lighten up can be a path toward deepening connections as joy finds its place in the living of each day.

Alchemy: From Type to Essence

Holy Source as Enlightened Spiritual Perspective

One of the primary illusions guiding this type is that they are separate from Source, from Holy Origin. They have been abandoned and left on this planet of insensitive humans. This highlights the Four's sensitivity to belonging. Feeling disconnected and misunderstood, Fours spend time seeking and longing for what is not present in the moment. Shifting attention to what is here for which they are grateful allows them to see the world anew.

When appreciating is the heart's posture, longing dissolves, and Fours discover they are the ones they have been seeking. Nothing is missing. Gratefulness gives rise to the virtue of equanimity, bringing a calm and steadiness that dissolves the illusion of abandonment. Holy Origin or Source is present, always has been, and forever will be, and we all are intimately connected to it. In this knowing, all of life—the peaks, valleys, and in between—are embraced in gratefulness. Comparisons fade, making space for joy to emerge. Fours understand and know in their bones that they belong and reside in the fabric of life. Magnified perceptions transform into a simple seeing as Fours find beauty in life's ordinariness and realize that at the core, all of life is holy, all extraordinary.

PRACTICES Bringing Awareness to Fours' Core Issues

Focused Inquiry

+ *How does the need to be unique and original impact your relationships?*
+ *When has your need for emotional depth been a barrier to your loving fully or connecting with others?*
+ *In what ways do you abandon yourself, your own heart? How might the longing you experience for something outside yourself actually be a longing for yourself?*
+ *What tells you that you're in performing mode? What allows you to return to your authentic self?*
+ *How might simplicity be a gateway to love?*

Our practices are ways of saying "yes" to our journey to our Essence.

Engagement to Counter the Type's Patterns

+ Notice when your mind goes into a comparing state. In these moments, bring something to mind for which you are grateful.

+ When you notice yourself over-engaging in a group or withdrawing, try shifting to simply being a part of the group without the need to be different. Notice if an inner sense of superiority or inferiority is driving the withdrawing or over-engaging. Inquire to see what's behind that.

+ Discern what really is your emotion and what is another's. Create a simple ritual to give back the other's emotions. This may be particularly helpful with your family of origin.

+ When you find yourself engaging in negative self-talk, remember the facts and focus on those rather than feelings. Notice if you're creating false narratives that influence you to take things personally. Drop the story and return to the facts.

+ Find ways to engage your creativity each day. Writing, acting, painting, creating altars—whatever form this takes, nurture it.

+ Create times of stillness to calm the mind and heart. Name specific people who supported you or situations that occurred during the day for which you're grateful.

Emotional depth seems authentic to Fours, who seek authenticity in themselves and others. Authenticity is present in the light-hearted moments of life, the simple delights that each day offers. To discover the authenticity in simplicity is to see the miraculous in the ordinary.

BEYOND OUR TYPE

When you see your authentic self, then you know that all you seek, you have. That which you long for is within you.

Sabbath-Keeping

Sabbath, in the traditional Jewish understanding, directs our focus to awe and provides space for us to cultivate delight in creation and our lives. Sabbath invites us to wake up to ourselves and our world.

This day is designed to honor the creative expression of Fours. Tapping into your creativity is energizing, and Fours tend to have an abundance of creative energy. Allow yourself to engage your mind, heart, and body in creative endeavors. Don't just think creatively; implement your creativity in some way. Write, draw, paint, make music, cook—create as you wish, but put your artistry in motion. When you notice your mind in a comparing mode, simply acknowledge it, then think of one thing you are grateful for and name that. Gratitude helps to diminish comparing states. As best you can, enter into a spirit of appreciation.

Cultivate appreciation for your life. Each Sabbath, take time to write a thank-you note to someone with whom you connected during the week, offering appreciation for the other. Write journal entries relating to your gratitude for specific people and events in the past week. Create an arrangement of gratitude for your home for the coming week, and allow it to be a symbol and reminder of your connection to Creative Source. On this day, you are neither too much nor not enough. Simply be who you are, and know that your being is just right. Create a ritual of gratitude for you!

A Type Four Prayer

In this present moment, I belong. Nothing is missing within me or beyond me. In this belonging, I open to the intimate connections that weave us together in the sacred web of life. Ground of Being, empty me of my shame and self-rejection and soften my comparing mind that I may know gratefulness for what I have and for who I am. May I be ever aware of the beauty and possibility that surrounds me, that is within me. Sacred Source of my life, ground me in the richness and the miracle in the ordinary, that it may guide me to the beauty in simplicity. From this "seeing" I know there really are no ordinary moments, for all is sacred in the holy web of belonging.

Head Types
Six, Five, Seven

First way of knowing: Logic, analysis, reason

Primary emotional issue: Fear

Orientation: Information

Energy: Detaching

Sensitivity: Being seen as incompetent

Growth: Attending to emotions

CHAPTER 10

The Power of Trusting: Type Six

Sixes are the most courageous type in the Enneagram, because they are aware of fear and keep going. Fear and doubt are well-known companions, yet when grounded, Sixes model a faith in themselves that beckons others to trust them. What does courage look like for you? As you read this chapter, invite your own type Six within to come forward.

TYPE SIX AT A GLANCE

Strengths: Anticipates well, friendly, poses insightful questions, logical, intuitive

Ego Ideal: I am loyal and connected.

Focus of Attention: Worst case

Motivation: To be safe by anticipating harm

Worldview: The world is dangerous and can't be trusted.

Fixation: Doubt

Vice: Fear

Holy Idea: Holy Faith

Virtue: Courage

Brief Overview

If I ever have to go to the emergency room, I'll be hoping for a type Six physician. Sixes are characterized by keen observation skills, logical thinking, curiosity, preparedness, and strong troubleshooting abilities. They're strong advocates for the underdog. Additionally, Sixes always want to know the "why" behind a symptom, decision, or action. Sixes' lack of self-trust is a part of what drives this need to ask why. Outside of crisis situations, Sixes are warm, witty, friendly, ask insightful questions, and excel at problem solving. At home, they can be determined, direct, as well as a bit bossy and stubborn. They can often intuit hidden agendas and tend to be the truth teller in groups.

Within each Six are two postures: phobic and counter-phobic. Sixes are both risk-averse and risk-taking. When the phobic or risk-averse part comes to the foreground, Sixes may adhere rigidly to rules, follow authority without question, and avoid conflict. They exude a warmth that engages others on friendly terms. The vice of fear can freeze a phobic Six. When the counter-phobic part emerges, Sixes push against fear. They may resist authority figures and behave counter to the status quo. Often, fear parades as anger in both the phobic and counter-phobic postures. Regardless of which posture is leading, both reside in every Six. When the vice of fear and Sixes' focus of attention on worst-case scenarios intersect, anxiety, worry, and mistrust arise.

While a focus on the worst can seem negative, considering potential trouble can work to ensure a positive outcome. In Sixes, worst-case thinking takes up residence in the head and is a constant; even that which is inconsequential may be seen through this lens. When I am asked to lead Enneagram workshops in other cities, I always hope that someone who leads with Six is on the planning committee. If so, I'm more confident that all the logistics will be thoughtfully and thoroughly considered. Good preparation usually leads to good outcomes. I remember leading a type Six panel several years ago where all of the participants were women, and they all brought their purses with them to the panel (of course, this isn't always the case!). I stifled a comment about trust, then boldly asked if they would mind sharing about some of the items they kept in their purses. True to the spirit of being prepared, everything but the kitchen sink was named!

Yet, this constant worst-case thinking, the *what if* questions and hesitating, are indicators that Sixes are moved by fear. When fearing the worst, uncertainty is unacceptable and increases Sixes' focus on the external. They lose sight of the wells of resources within as feelings of helplessness and doubt arise. In these moments, Sixes lack trust in themselves and may give away their own power and authority to others. They can feel as if they have no inner ground on which to stand and may have a sense of falling. Researching and seeking answers from others are common behaviors when making decisions. Sixes want to be sure about their decisions. Issues of safety and security can dominate their thinking, and this drives a desire for predictability and certainty.

Making friends with uncertainty is key inner work for this type. As spiritual teacher Eckhart Tolle put it, "The Roman philosopher Tacitus rightly observed that 'The desire for safety stands against every great and noble enterprise.' If uncertainty is unacceptable to you, it turns into fear. If it is perfectly acceptable, it turns into increased aliveness, alertness, and creativity."[1] For those of us who love Sixes, a **compassionate entry point** can be offering the simple questions, "How is not knowing a gift?" and "What is a potential positive outcome of uncertainty?"

An interesting feature of Sixes is their self-trust that arises in a crisis. It seems that worry and anxiety manifest not in times of trouble, but in the anticipation of what is to come when the doubting mind asks, "What can go awry?" Self-trust is elusive when there is time to anticipate. Yet, when an unexpected crisis arises and there's no time to think, Sixes act decisively and seem to know intuitively how to respond. They observe quickly, taking in people and scenarios, noticing the slightest nuances in facial expressions and shifts in patterns. Their logical minds solve problems fast, and we all follow the Sixes! It's highly probable that type Six is the most observant Enneagram type. Sixes are difficult to surprise, but oddly, the type most averse to surprise may be the type best able to function when surprised.

Most of the time, Sixes' observation skills are mental and lack attention to the body's sensations. Sensations help us ground ourselves in the present moment and allow for clarity of thinking. Exercising helps to lower the mental energy down into the body and end the mind's future-orientation. Recently, I learned from a Six that running on a track doesn't help her get more present, but running on a forest trail where she has to focus on rocks and roots so she doesn't trip enables her to be present in the moment. Along with exercising, I've noticed that it seems helpful for Sixes to use their hands. Activities like writing, painting, woodworking, weaving, and drumming all support coming back to the present moment.

The Striving and the Avoidance

When projects, tasks, or relationships falter, the inner critic haunts Sixes by directing their thinking to "I should have known. I should have been more prepared." To avoid trouble and to be well prepared, Sixes have their fingers in all of the pies, so to speak. A mistrust of others and of life's unfolding drives Sixes to over-function and over-think. Striving to know the outcome ahead of time and to avoid uncertainty opens the door for anxiety and worry. As an information-oriented type, Sixes continually seek to learn the "why," usually looking for answers outside themselves. Keeping an external focus distances Sixes from their own wealth of knowledge, life experiences, and intuition. When asked by Sixes for our opinions, a **compassionate entry point** is to ask them in response, "If you were me, what would you tell yourself?" This question is a good reminder that Sixes really do know possible solutions and can trust themselves.

Striving for certainty is exhausting because it's future-oriented and keeps vigilant scanning alive. Constantly living beyond the present and pre-thinking is wearing. For Sixes, having a plan is important, and certainty feels safe. As Dr. Daniels, a type Six himself, used to remind us, "Sixes replace trust with certainty." If you lead with type Six, you might ask yourself, *"When is my grasp for certainty most strong? How might I reimagine uncertainty?"* Relating to the previously mentioned quote from Tolle, when uncertainty is welcomed, it can lead to a kind of clearing out of that which we have outgrown. The ego doesn't navigate uncertainty well, so it drives Sixes to scurry around until they can wrangle something certain. Yet, when uncertainty is welcomed, it invites quiet stillness and a time of listening with the heart that can be a birthing ground for the new to come forward.

The defense mechanism for Sixes is projection. Projection means that we attribute to others what we are blind to in ourselves, whether negative or positive. Sixes often project the mistrust they have of themselves onto others. Projecting their own power and authority is common as well. Discerning between projection and intuition can clear a path for returning to the self. Clear replaces fear when Sixes trust the gift of their own intuition. Keep in mind that projections have emotions attached to them. Intuition has a neutral, simple tone. The more Sixes project, the more they feel abandoned and alone.

The Core Fear and the Pivot

The worldview of Sixes is that the world is a dangerous place, and to be alone in such a world feels scary and unsafe. Being alone or abandoned is a core fear, and some Sixes will stay in relationships because it brings an element of safety. A grasping to connect with others may indicate how unsafe they feel inside themselves. Loyalty arises from this fear of being alone as Sixes believe, "If I'm loyal to you, then you'll be loyal to me, thus I'll feel safe." However, when Sixes are less loyal to themselves than they are to others, resentment can arise. Resentment is a clue that Sixes are abandoning themselves. Inner work for this type that focuses on attending to their own needs and wants can be healing. The practice of being more loyal to self than to others is work that grows all of us.

Shifting the focus from the external to the inner landscape is an important first step. Sixes' lack of trust is birthed in the belief that they have no inner foundation, no Ground within themselves on which to stand. This is untrue, of course, but it feels true to Sixes, especially young Sixes. It takes courage to make this inward turn, and when the virtue of courage arises, self-trust emerges. Keep in mind that strength is not courage. If you lead with type Six, how do you discern the difference between them?

Remembering good decisions and past successes can be helpful for this type in claiming a trust in self. A **compassionate entry point** for Sixes is sharing with them our witness of their good decisions and successes.

For all of us, the ability to trust indicates a stance on inner ground and an awakened heart. The courage to step into uncertainty, to move through doubting and fearful times, is a grounded, openhearted response to life. Paradoxically, it is not certainty but uncertainty that leads us to trust. Uncertainty is the perfect teacher in the school of trust, and making friends with uncertainty is a key development process for Sixes. When Sixes have the courage to look within and find and stand on their inner ground, feelings of groundlessness shift as Sixes claim their power and trust themselves. This trust leads to acceptance of life as it is, as well the unfolding of life that is to come. Fear dissolves. Self-trust is.

Sixes: *The only preparation needed is within—a grounded presence, a curious mind, and an open heart.*

Companion Voices

As you read the stories from the companion writers, be open to finding a part of you in their shared experiences.

Beth, our next contributor, speaks to the leadership and strengths of Sixes in times of crisis. Taking a stand and trusting her intuition, she perseveres with her daughter's chronic health issues as she embodies what it means to be an advocate.

It should come as no surprise with my type's "worst-case scenario" thinking that most of the time, I bemoan the fact that I lead with type Six. It is so easy to focus on the negative attributes and worry about all the flaws and things that need to be fixed. The need to fix things and secure my environment is the lens through which I see the world. Why not see myself this way too when I look in the mirror or read my latest "Enneathought of the Day"? When one of these insights drops into my email inbox and says I am "indecisive, anxious, and complaining," I feel exposed in both an uncomfortable and an exhilarating way. I vacillate between *"It's over. I'll never be whole."* and *"Wow, that's a truth I can do something about."*

But then, I am reminded of the benefits of my hyper-vigilant and hyper-improvement scan. I intend the better not just for myself but for others. I realize that I may need to modulate this vigilance when it comes to employee reviews, giving editorial feedback, or being asked my honest opinion by friends, as it can come across as a bit harsh. I also believe these traits are necessary in times of crisis and advocacy.

The quick scan of the type Six allows me to see potential weaknesses, think through consequences logically, sort through various plans, and choose the best. Now that I have lived through several national crises and a few familial ones, I understand how quickly I can take up a "can do" attitude. When others are paralyzed, angry, or pessimistic, I demonstrate the ability to focus on the positive possibilities in a crisis or time of transition.

When the world is spinning, my mind is not. I can drop deeply into my intuition and find the next best course of action. The way my consciousness can hold a broad awareness of my surroundings with a focused awareness of my next step helped me respond immediately to the events of September 11, 2001, as a resident of lower Manhattan. I partnered with friends to mobilize supplies and catering to aid and feed the rescue workers that were searching for survivors. For my type Six self, sleeping and serving at Ground Zero felt like the calmest place to be in the storm of grief, rage, and conspiracy, as I was able to be with others sorting through the debris and looking for a way through. Similarly, when Covid 19 began to shut down workplaces, schools, and houses of worship, I quickly set about creating alternative plans of action for my work, family, and church. As scary and sad as it was, the first few months felt like an opportunity to try new things and reevaluate old patterns and systems that might need improving. While others expressed panic, I felt prepared and purposeful, with room to carry others along.

As much as I get frustrated with my anxious mind and insomniac patterns in times of "normalcy," I do appreciate how my habit of heightened observation and ability to ask questions that others don't think to ask prepare me to be calm and centered in a crisis. I also appreciate the trust granted to me by others when we do hit these rough spots. Then, I experience what it is like to trust myself while also feeling the trust that others have placed in me all along but that I am often unable to absorb due to my incessant doubting mind.

"Everyone should have an advocate," I heard one patient say to another in one of the many hospital waiting rooms that I have frequented as a mother of a medically compromised child and as a pastor. They were particularly talking about the arena of healthcare, but I heard in that phrase something I deeply long for and desire for others. After a prolonged pandemic exposed again the systemic problems that continue to tear our social fabric, I have found a wider acceptance of this term, *advocate*, in people's personal and social worldviews. I've also discovered how the instincts of the Six can be harnessed toward advocacy for the good rather than devolving into complaining without problem solving.

I've felt this need for advocacy most keenly in my role as a mother to a child with chronic health conditions and a history of medical fragility and tracheostomy dependency. The realities of healthcare within a system of private insurance create a system under the strain of uncoordinated medical specialties and providers, inflated costs, and lack of transparency.

I have come to accept and been told by many of my daughter's providers that I am the expert on her as a patient. Therefore, I come to every appointment armed with her most recent records. Because of the long recollection of my type, I can recite these by memory. I am always amazed at how often I must correct something in their database or electronic chart, as if she and I were being seen as patients for the first time. I employ all of my type's attention to detail, ability to foresee potential pitfalls, and logical approach to problem solving in every medical visit. For this reason, I've been able to refuse certain procedures and suggest more moderate approaches to the healing of her airway, which have in the long run preserved her independent living skills. Rather than treating my questions as antagonistic, doctors have responded to my research and resolve to follow through with at-home therapies as cooperative and collaborative. More than once, I've been told they trusted me with alternatives to surgery that they wouldn't suggest for other less reliable caregivers or patients. The system is rife with distrust between patients, doctors, and insurance companies. This is a source of sadness for me but also a call to action, both as a patient advocate and a social activist. As I recoup time spent on the former, I hope to dedicate more time to the latter and to solving the more systemic problems that plague our healthcare system.

Being an advocate has extended a feeling I've felt as a crisis responder, which is that of standing in my power and not giving it away. The virtues of courage and faith are deep within the core of type Six, and yet often they are the hardest to access as anything more than a fleeting intuition or sudden conviction to act or not back down. I am still learning how to manage my type structure so I can show up more assured and faithful . . . not just to myself but also to others.

Beth reminds us that Sixes are calm when "the world is spinning." And she offers a beautiful example of a type Six advocate, one whose observation skills, mental acuity, and love for her daughter have made and continue to make an impact. Fear and faith hold hands in her advocacy, clearing a path for the possible.

Cathy, our next contributor, identifies as a lesbian and shares some of her experiences as a young, imaginative Six and the gifts of scanning that kept her safe. In various roles throughout life, her inner observer has been alert, noticing when her type was constricting or expanding her.

Being exposed to the Narrative Tradition of the Enneagram in 2018, it was as if scales had fallen from my eyes. For most of my adult life, I've worked on myself through Al Anon, therapy, prayer, meditation, etc., resulting in many positive changes. I was in a very good place until 2017 when, after only five years of marriage (and being together for seven years) my wife "Pete" died. This event rended my heart and soul like nothing before, and so I walked into my first Enneagram workshop with Sandra a wounded person. While I had been aware of who I was and where my challenges lie, this new me was especially receptive to what was being presented through the Enneagram. My perspective broadened; all the work I had done on myself seemed to reach fruition when viewed through the Enneagram lens.

I am a 62-year-old white lesbian who is an Episcopal priest. The priesthood was a second career that I entered after 20-plus years as a psychotherapist working in community mental health settings. I'd been ordained 10 years when my wife died (somewhat suddenly) after a brief, brutal battle with lung cancer. In 2018, when I was first introduced to the Enneagram, not only was I reeling from the death of my wife, but a new Bishop had changed my position on his staff, giving me a new title and many new colleagues. On top of this, my 91-year-old mother's health was rapidly deteriorating, and I was moving from the country back into the city. The losses were huge, and as someone who leads with type Six, the uncertainty in most areas of my life was excruciating. Everything I thought anchored me—people and circumstances—had been upended.

I had no idea who I was in this new reality.

Therein lies the rub: my circumstances were definitely new, but my core self was unchanged. It wasn't different, it wasn't changed. It was still me, but my expression of me? That was different. Where I used to feel courageous and sure-footed, I was now paralyzed by fear and unsure of where I stood, aching to have something to hold on to. My faith did not waver. As a matter of fact, it kept me from falling headlong into the abyss. In this state of uncertainty, I was introduced to Sandra and the Enneagram.

As someone who leads with type Six, I tend to prepare for every possibility with worst-case scenario planning. But how does one rely on that very familiar behavior when the worst-case scenario happened and you found yourself wholly unprepared for it? As someone who was raised in an alcoholic home, I was good at scanning the mood of the house when I came home. Was Mom available, or was she angry with my father and turning into her inward rage that she thought she hid from us kids? Would Dad come home that night? Did I want him to (because then there would be a fight) or not (because then there would be more silent rage from Mom)? As a young adult, when I came to embrace my identity as lesbian, I would scan constantly, on guard against being called a dyke, or stared or smirked at. I was always on guard. As an outsider of mainstream America, I am always scanning the horizon for an attack, a slur, a stare, or a sneer.

This hyper-vigilance served me as a child. I knew when to stay out of the house or hide with my sisters upstairs. As a young adult I was someone friends always came to in a crisis because I knew what was happening and I knew—I just *knew*—what needed to be done. People felt safe around me, even if I never felt safe with myself.

My first career was as a psychotherapist. I was very good in this role and found it satisfying, but it was never my dream vocation. As a little girl (a flat-out "tomboy" who longed to wear football pajamas and fantasized on the playground that I was playing third base for the Chicago Cubs in the seventh game of the World Series), when people asked me what I wanted to be when I grew up, I would say "a teacher." I didn't want to be a teacher, but I hailed from a long line of teachers so it seemed the right thing to say. The truth was I wanted to be an Episcopal priest, but I dared not say that in the late 1960s and '70s because that was not a career that women were "allowed" to pursue. And being a gay woman? Forget it. I didn't fit in anyplace. I wasn't a girl in the 1960s paradigm; everything I was interested in was "boy stuff." I was constantly on alert about being teased, ridiculed, and shamed.

As I grew, I tried to fit in. I tried to "look like a girl." I couldn't look like a traditional girl because I wasn't one. Who I felt I was wasn't acceptable to the outside world, therefore it wasn't acceptable to me. All I wanted to do was fit in. All I *could* do was not fit in. Most days I'm not that different from the third base–playing, dungaree-wearing athletic "tomboy" who, if I haven't been exercising, praying, and breathing deeply, wants to be anything but who I truly am . . .

How have I moved from fear to courage? From longing to fit in to being secure in who it is the Creator made me to be? From "I'm all alone" to "I have myself to lean on"? By looking within and finding the ground that is strong enough to hold me and has always been there. By pushing myself physically so that I stay in my body instead of in some catastrophic future. By remembering that it is me who has survived and thrived through it all.

When I trust myself, I trust others with clarity and wisdom, trusting those who are trustworthy and protecting myself (without losing myself) from those who are not. I can sense a phony from 20 paces. The problem is that I don't always trust that inner sense. I doubt it, reject it, push it away . . . and when I do, I get in trouble.

When I lose myself—forgetting my body, forgetting that I stand on my own firm foundation—I become reactive and exhibit poor judgment. When I do that, often the "worst-case scenario" comes true. I waver, I forget, and I lose myself in the mess that isn't mine. I call this being reactive instead of responsive. When I am reactive, I catastrophize things; the catastrophe I imagined comes true to a certain extent. When I am responsive, I take what is presented, notice what my initial reaction (physically and emotionally) is, and then let my body move through reaction and (usually by moving my body and deepening my breathing) settle into responding.

To be able to do that requires that I watch what I eat, get enough sleep, breathe in fresh air, elevate my heart rate through physical exercise, and remind myself that I am beloved by the Creator, so therefore I must be beloved by me as well. I need to do all these things regularly, consistently, and intentionally. When I do that, I get closer to my Essence.

I love leading with type Six because I love being aware, ready and able to take in all that is happening around me, to navigate it and move a group of people through the chaos and into what is meant to be. For that is what I have done and continue to do: move through the chaos of an ungrounded self and into the roundedness of what is meant to be.

Cathy's story reminds us that the characteristics of our type can be both gift and curse. She makes the powerful point that trust in others begins with trust in self. Through life's losses, she leans into self-care and her body for support and to remember that she has Ground.

Alchemy: From Type to Essence

Holy Faith as Enlightened Spiritual Perspective

The path of growth for Sixes lies in trusting that they have inner strength that arises from their own Ground of Being. This trust supports the inward turn. This trust is the birthplace of courage. When

Sixes find the courage to turn inward and know they can count on themselves, faith in self, in others, and in the great Mystery arises. In this faith, Sixes realize that they are held in the holy web of life. Connection is a given. There is no need for anticipation. Sixes can trust in the unfolding of their lives and remember how the world has befriended them. The "I should have known" narrative vanishes in the presence of Holy Faith. The only preparation needed is to arrive in the now and root in their inner Ground of Being.

Just as we know the sky is star-filled in daylight and the sun still burns even when hidden by clouds, we can trust, without evidence, that our Essence is solidly within us this day and for all the days to come. We need only to lean into it knowing this Ground supports us as we step forward, without predictability, in a world of surprises.

PRACTICES Bringing Awareness to Sixes' Core Issues

Focused Inquiry

+ *When has the need for certainty been a barrier to your loving fully?*
+ *What supports you in being more loyal to yourself than to others or to an organization?*
+ *How are you distracting yourself with little things so as not to birth your dream?*
+ *When do you trust yourself? What is the outcome of your self-trust?*
+ *What are the clues that you have moved into the future, and what supports you in returning to the present moment?*

Our practices are ways of saying "yes" to our journey to our Essence.

Engagement to Counter the Type's Patterns

+ Notice when worst-case thinking is in operation and invite positive possibilities to balance it.
+ Where do you feel steady, safe, and secure in your body? In times of anxiety, try shifting your attention there.
+ Each week, reflect on your personal success stories, remembering times when your action, your decision, was the right course. Feel this in your body when you lack confidence. Then name someone who may seek your advice.
+ Find ways to use your hands, in whatever form you prefer (writing, painting, knitting, playing guitar).
+ Exercise each day, if possible, in order to lower the energy from your head down into your body.

Scanning and future-tripping remove Sixes from the present. Returning to "right now" lessens anxiety and doubt. Presence clears the mind. When Sixes replace preparation with presence, they have access to their own power to be. Clarity comes.

BEYOND YOUR TYPE

All you need is within yourself, including the faith that you are held in life's seamless web of interconnections.

Sabbath-Keeping

Sabbath, in the traditional Jewish understanding, directs our focus to awe and provides space for us to cultivate delight in creation and our lives. Sabbath invites us to wake up to ourselves and our world.

This day is designed to nourish the senses and lessen the need for "evidence" on which to act or make meaning—no need to ask why. Create a sacred space with icons and symbols that remind you of your own strengths as well as your connections with others. Pray in the ways that are most comfortable for you. Prayer settles us into a larger context, allowing us to better understand our interdependence with All. This is a day to be in the body. Hiking, swimming, dancing, and singing can ease over-thinking. During Sabbath, practice making decisions without all the information you think you need. Wing it and trust that the outcome will be friendly. Note your sensations and feel emotions in the moment. Notice when your mind goes to worst-case thinking and use your quick wit to playfully shift to best-case thinking. Go lightly this day. Rest your worries, your fears, your anticipation. Settle into each moment without the need to prepare for anything.

Take this day to reflect on all that has gone well in the past week and on all the moments when you trusted yourself to know what to do. These moments are evidence of your own authority and power. Celebrate that.

A Type Six Prayer

Ground of my Being, you are my foundation, and you create in me a refuge for trusting myself. As I claim my Ground, trust arises and my suspicions fade. Empty me of my anxieties, doubts, and fearful imaginings. Remind me of my inner resources and power. Knowing that steady Ground is within me, I move forward in an uncertain world. Guide me as I travel the path of courage so I may lean into myself when the waters are troubled, having faith in the unfolding, growing myself into my own authority. Hold me in the fearful times, hold me in the fearless times. In this Ground of my Being, I rise to offer my full and powerful self in each moment.

CHAPTER 11

The Power of Engaging: Type Five

Fives are the most private type in the Enneagram and the least spontaneous. Their pullback energy is powerful when scarcity dominates their thinking. When touched by life's abundance, Fives' generosity knows no bounds. Abundance or scarcity? Each of us, no matter our type, navigates which of these two moves us. As you read this chapter, consider the Five within you.

TYPE FIVE AT A GLANCE

Strengths: Analytical, curious, pragmatic, thorough

Ego Ideal: I am knowledgeable.

Focus of Attention: Detaching and observing for possible intrusions

Motivation: To maintain privacy and boundaries

Worldview: The world is demanding and depleting.

Fixation: Stinginess

Vice: Avarice

Holy Idea: Holy Omniscience

Virtue: Non-attachment

Brief Overview

Fives are undemanding people. Usually calm and nonreactive, Fives seek to understand the "why" of situations. Naturally curious, they appreciate learning and researching for information, diving into the minutiae of the topic that currently holds their interest. Problem solving is a delightful pastime, and reading in a quiet space is heaven. Fives are people of facts and can surprise us with the amount of information they have stored. You want a Five on your team when playing Trivial Pursuit!

With a subtle humor and an analytical mind, Fives are fascinating to engage with and are accessible when they trust that the other isn't overly demanding. Believing that inner detaching keeps them safe from being depleted, Fives scan the environment for who or what may be intrusive and draining. Yet, depletion doesn't necessarily arise from external factors. Fives can deplete themselves by over-thinking and pre-thinking. They move into the future to attempt to figure things out before they occur. This premeditation prevents them from landing in their own experience of the moment and serves as a barrier to deepening relationships. When detached, Fives have difficulty experiencing emotion and may think about emotions rather than feeling them, waiting until they are alone or with a trusted significant other to allow their emotions to surface. As Dr. Daniels used to say, "Fives substitute information for emotion."

It isn't that Fives aren't capable of strong feelings. Certainly, they can be. However, much of their energy is used to contain, contract, and censor. When Fives lessen their mental activity and ground themselves in their bodies, they have more energy available to experience feelings and emotions in the now, without pulling away to analyze. Analyzing feels familiar, while emotions seem chaotic and unpredictable. Accessing the wisdom of the heart may be foreign to this type. That which resides in the heart—gratefulness, desires, passion—can, at times, seem out of reach.

This doesn't rule out the fun and adventure that Fives seek and enjoy, whether alone or with others. They can be fun playmates, and they appreciate new experiences. In vigorous adventures, engaging the body more allows some of the Five's self-containment to dissolve. Embodiment brings an aliveness!

Fives are sensitive to being seen as incompetent, so they are thorough with their facts. This sensitivity drives Fives to withdraw to think things over before speaking, deciding, or acting. The opportune moment may elude Fives who remain in analysis mode too long and frustrate others who are left without needed information. A good practice for Fives is to communicate when they will share their thoughts and to practice offering more information than they think is needed. In a working environment, a type Five manager or leader may not offer necessary information or support to those they lead, projecting onto others the Five's desire to solve problems independently. Note to Fives: communicate more than you think you need to!

Valuing privacy, people who lead with Five seek time alone each day to renew themselves and mentally sort out their day. The vice of avarice keeps Fives holding on to resources they believe will maintain their privacy and autonomy. Additionally, avarice creates blinders to abundance and maintains a mental framework of scarcity. Coming from this place of scarcity, Fives rarely initiate conversations or connections. A **compassionate entry point** for those who love Fives is to keep initiating and inviting, even when the Fives don't reciprocate the initiating. Five is a withdrawing, private, and contained type. Initiating rarely comes up on their radar.

A fear of "not enough" narrows Fives' perspective so much so that generosity may go unnoticed. Thus, they may rarely offer appreciation or a thank you. Allowing themselves to be extravagant is a good practice for Fives, as it offers a sense of abundance. Buy the best chocolates, purchase that kayak, or host a dinner party! Notice when scarcity is in the driver's seat. Indications that scarcity is operating are revealed by the thought, "I can do without that." When engagement with friends lessens or withholding information increases, notice if scarcity is driving these behaviors.

Grounding in and attuning to the body supports Fives in lessening the mental focus on scarcity. Exercising, bubble baths, dancing, and chanting are all good activities to lower the energy from the head down into the body. When grounded in our bodies, we can't be overwhelmed.

The Striving and the Avoidance

For Fives, striving for more information is a constant. Information supports greater understanding. Fives love to learn, and many Fives continue their education, attaining more degrees and credentials throughout their lives. For this type especially, knowledge is power. Holding a secret or having knowledge that others don't can feel powerful. In this power mode, Fives seem to think they can figure things out and solve any problem on their own, as long as they can access more or different information. Asking for help or support is anathema due to their sensitivity to being seen as incompetent. Of course, no one will think this of Fives, but this sensitivity is the foundational support for the striving to be self-reliant.

Self-reliance is prized by Fives, but while it works to a point, the more Fives retract and rely on themselves the more isolated they become, thinking themselves into a corner. We need more than our own perspective! To think otherwise leads to arrogance. If you lead with type Five, remember a time when being self-reliant narrowed your perspective and led to difficult times. What did you notice about yourself in these times? Ask yourself, *"What helps me lessen my grasping for self-reliance?"*

The defense mechanism of isolation of affect keeps Fives in the head, where they feel safe, and distant from emotions. Emotions cloud thinking, or so Fives believe. This lack of affect or expression can imply a strong intellect as well as hiding Fives' fear. This defense further isolates them. While Fives love their time alone, it's important to recognize when alone time becomes "most of the time." When our beloved Fives seem more withdrawn than usual, offering opportunities for brief connections can be a **compassionate entry point** and show of support. Remember, Fives will not ask for this, but small, noninvasive acts of kindness will let Fives know they aren't alone.

The Core Fear and the Pivot

Fives see the world as overly demanding and thus depleting. They anticipate being drained or sucked dry by life, so they engage with caution. A fear of depletion drives these responses. This fear keeps emotions at a distance and minimizes connection with others. Yet, as mentioned previously, Fives' own tendency toward analysis and pre-thinking depletes them. Attempting to know the outcome beforehand or preparing to respond to potential questions or problems places Fives in the future and keeps the mind activated. A fear of emptiness, of not having enough information, amplifies the grasping for more. Information is a false security blanket. Real security comes from returning to presence and landing fully in the body. The body anchors us in the present. When Fives are present, feeling emotions is as natural as thinking thoughts. Neither is draining.

Healing begins when Fives reach out to others for support instead of attempting to find solutions on their own. More thinking and more information are dead ends. Oddly, when Fives allow themselves to ask for help, it demonstrates a trust in themselves. This self-trust reveals the illusion of self-reliance. Asking for help doesn't lessen us when we trust ourselves and know our limitations. A supportive practice for Fives is to ask for help in small ways each week. It will feel foreign at first, but with more practice, an ease in receiving others' support is born. In this ease, connections deepen. The virtue of non-attachment emerges as Fives realize that there is strength in interdependency. We need each other, and we are not separate beings. Fives' virtue of non-attachment brings an openhanded response to life, inviting their generous heart to open as scarcity leaves the premises. In non-attachment, Fives release their grip on self-reliance and share themselves with others.

Fives: *Why live as if you have something to lose? The world is generous. Dive in!*

Companion Voices

As you read the stories from the companion writers, be open to finding a part of you in their shared experiences.

The shift from withdrawing to engaging is the focus of our next contributor, **Nicole**, who describes her struggles to balance relationships and family life with her need for alone time.

I thought I was simply a perfectionist, a pessimistic loner. As a young person, then a young adult, I didn't care how others felt because my mission was to protect myself from people who could potentially hurt and deplete me. Then I became a wife and, a couple of years after, a mother. At that point in life, I quickly learned that the loner in me had to be fed. That was easier said than done, because I had people who depended on me and required my protection. So, for the next 21 years, I battled myself, starving for alone time, not because I didn't love my family, but because I rarely had opportunities to refuel. My routine often left me feeling smothered. Feeling this way invited resentment. After all, isn't a wife and mother supposed to take care of her husband and children without feelings of resentment? Well, the smothering would become resentment and, of course, the resentment would become guilt. The guilt left me constantly questioning myself as well as my faith. I struggled to find balance between caring for those I love and making time for self-care—to find relaxation, peace, and quiet.

I am often misunderstood. People think I am uncaring and insensitive—even people I love. I don't try to convince them otherwise because it's easier for me to bear that burden than to appear weak or frail. Prior to learning the characteristics of an Enneagram Five, I believed that people misunderstood me because we live in a society and culture in which women—especially Black women—cannot be considered confident and capable. Instead of capable, I have been labeled arrogant, insensitive, brash . . . even rude and unsympathetic. Most often I've felt this way in my professional life. I am not the most visibly sensitive person, but I care deeply and I am emotional. While I can easily share feelings of delight and joy, other emotions, such as sadness and anger, are more difficult. I believe my brain simply works better when my emotional self is in check. I cannot process or accomplish next steps or goals if I am not thinking clearly. One of the illusions of type Five is that emotions confuse thinking. Therefore, I may seem aloof.

At times, when I return home to my family, I still feel so self-contained that I cannot freely express my emotional self. This contained emotion is a result of personal expectations to be my best and achieve the most within my family. Failure on the home front is not an option, and my Five structure tells me that emotions can undermine my efforts. I am confident in my roles at home because what I do there, I do alone.

Cooking, organizing, and care-giving are a part of who I am as a wife and mother.

So today, as a 41-year-old Black woman, contrary to everything I thought I knew about myself, I'm learning more about me. I'm exploring my hardwiring, my inner landscape—not what makes me tick, but why I tick the way I do. This experience has been eye-opening. It has given me a spirit of freedom similar to when I changed my lifestyle to live a Christ-centered life. Learning about the characteristics of an Enneagram Five has given me clarity as well as more self-confidence. Additionally, knowing that my Essence, who I am beyond my type, is so beautiful allows me to accept my fear, reservation, and need to gather information rather than judge it.

I have typically identified myself in my relationship to my community, culture, family, and friends. Hearing the same descriptions of myself over the years, especially from people whose opinions I respect and cherish, has caused me to second-guess myself. Some labels were negative, but I chose to accept them and live as if it was just the way I was. My personal motto was "Love me or leave me, I am who I am." I grew up loving myself; I was taught that I was enough just as I am. So, I believed the loner, the pessimist, and the perfectionist in me were okay—were enough. I wore my labels like masks. If I did not want to be bothered, I displayed unfriendliness. When unsure of people and surroundings, I displayed brashness and arrogance. These labels kept me safely in my comfort zone, distant and private. More importantly, my behavior kept unwanted people out of my space. In fact, I grew to love it because I love my alone time and my ability to keep people at a safe distance. My sad reality, however, was that my marriage, at times, suffered because of my great desire to be who I identified myself as being. It has been easier to be the self-reliant loner than a feeling and transparent woman who shares her true feelings and intimate needs with her husband, children, parents, and inner circle.

In the past, I told people that I am a work in progress. Now I am learning to be cautiously optimistic. I have always believed that change is positive. However, I have not always easily engaged in change because it pushes me out of my comfort zone of predictability and automatic patterns. I am learning to open my heart center and be expressive. Rather than avoiding or limiting moments that cause fear, I am learning to move toward those moments, open and free to the idea of expressing my emotions. Rather than pre-thinking, I'm living in the moment. This openness has allowed my family to see me as a caring, more human person. The walls I've built over time to protect me are melting away. I lean on my husband and children. In a sense, I am becoming less self-reliant. I am opening myself up so my family can aid and assist me, just as I aid and assist them. I'm open to risks and new experiences. This openness arises from learning that I am truly enough.

While I am sometimes pessimistic, I am also processing and seeking ways to make things better. I am seeing a bigger picture. I've learned I need alone time to refuel, recharge, and ground myself. My grounding practices are simply the things I enjoy, like quiet time, prayer, and reading scripture. These things help me be present. In presence, I can be both open and inviting and still process what's next.

It's been scary, unnerving, and amazingly refreshing to learn more about the aspects of my type Five structure. Frankly, it's become easier to love myself and believe "I am okay" and "I am enough." I am learning not to deplete myself by trying to make my world predictable. I am more complete because fear does not hinder me in the same ways. I am opening more and more to my heart, allowing and expressing my emotions.

Claiming her "enoughness" while courageously dissolving self-reliance has been life-changing for Nicole. Risking not knowing ahead of time brings more surprise and delight to life. She has more energy for those who are beloved to her.

Marilyn, our next contributor, discusses the scarcity issue for Fives, along with the ways her sharp mind has allowed her to participate more fully in life.

As an 85-year-old white woman living in a small, Southern city, I first encountered the Enneagram in the early '90s and struggled to identify my type. Type Five was presented as a masculine image of an engineer or a scientist, and I did not relate to that—although I did identify ways that I was not the other types. I did not continue with the studies. My interest returned to the Enneagram at a Narrative Enneagram conference in Montreat, North Carolina, in 2005. Guided by the descriptive paragraphs in *The Essential Enneagram* as well as panel discussions, I began to explore the possibility of leading with type Five. I was certain I was part of the head triad since I was often unaware of my body, especially as I busied myself with my career, and did not trust my heart.

My identification as one who leads with Five was confirmed the following year when I returned to the Montreat Enneagram conference and sat on a panel with three women who also identify with type Five. We bonded quickly. The characteristic I identified with most was the tendency to withhold my energy, knowledge, and feelings. We also discussed our common tendency to sit back and observe new situations before deciding to join in or to not participate. Even when we did make a choice to participate, we tended to think long and hard before expressing ourselves. On the Five panel, we tried to convey that our feelings were powerful and deep within us; it was just difficult to express them to others, even those to whom we were close. This tends to frustrate those with whom we are in relationships.

I grew up as the only child of parents whose lives had been significantly impacted by the economic hardships of the 1920s and '30s in the South. It worked well for me to be an independent child who was easily entertained by picture books and began to read before starting school. I was told that my first and frequent sentence was "I will do it myself!" Suitable as this was in my home, it did not serve me well as I entered the years of adolescence. I began to realize that I did not have a clue about how to navigate making the deep friendships for which I longed. I compensated by being a good student and finding my voice by participating in the debate team.

If the social scene of high school was confusing, the complexity of navigating the prestigious university I chose was overwhelming. In the '50s, the socially acceptable way of escaping such a situation with some dignity was to get married. So, I did. Three children and 10 years later, I returned to college, then graduate school, to prepare for what became a very satisfying career as a school psychologist and part-time college instructor. As I approached midlife, I divorced, and my children began their adult lives. I was now able to focus on *me* and get in touch with my spiritual self, which had long been dormant.

During the years that followed, I began an exciting and heady exploration of liberal theology. Mentoring small groups, studying spiritual writings, traveling to attend workshops and hear the leading writers of the era, and going on pilgrimages to England and Europe were ways that I nurtured my soul. Amid this whirlwind of activity, I was startled by a friend's comment: "You are so busy learning about God that you are not experiencing God." I have reflected on this over the years and now am beginning to understand that the most meaningful times for me were, and still are, in the quiet moments of a loving connection with a friend, a simple interaction with nature, an unanticipated moment of awe, and the fleeting awareness of the Oneness of all.

I am discovering that it is not a theology that I was seeking, but something beyond words, facts, and logic, which cannot be found by searching. A butterfly might come and sit on my shoulder if I sit quietly without expectation. Such moments are best experienced without trying to capture and define them. For me, these experiences are best expressed by loving action in the world, even small gestures of encouragement that may seem insignificant. If words must be used, perhaps C.S. Lewis's book title, *Surprised by Joy*, would suffice.

For one who leads with Five, my healthy shift is from scarcity to openheartedness, from withholding to trust, and from fear to peace with myself and others. Insights from Enneagram teachings remind me to shift attention to my body to feel emotion and stay in the present without future concerns. This allows me to focus on a meaningful response to a situation instead of withholding my opinion or information. Beginning and ending each day with a gratitude practice supports my awareness of abundance and helps me stay open and positive.

Can I stay in this place all of the time? Of course not, I'm human. But I have experienced joy that encourages me to continue seeking experiences that enhance my life. Had I known when I was young what I know now about my Enneagram type, it would have prevented much worry and fret, but I believe that every twist and turn of the journey contributed to my positive aging. I believe that each person has a path with peaks and valleys and the task for each of us is, in an individual and unique way, to explore and appreciate the landscape of the journey.

Engaging in "butterfly moments" and being open to surprise brings wisdom that information cannot. Marilyn's journey from withdrawing to gratefulness is a testament to her belief in abundance. In her aging, appreciation and acceptance have emerged in powerful ways. May it be so for us all.

Alchemy: From Type to Essence

Holy Omniscience as Enlightened Spiritual Perspective

Fives deny being fully themselves when they isolate, withdraw, and contract. Exploring engaging as an entry point to deepening their capacity to give and receive love opens Fives to the possibility of not knowing ahead of time. When we engage in the moment, we risk sharing ourselves and our feelings without the benefit of a predictable outcome. It is possible that this moment may drain us. Also, it is possible that we will become more of who we are. It's worth the risk. Not risking engagement dooms us to a shriveled life.

When Fives see through their enlightened spiritual perspective of Holy Omniscience, a full knowing that includes wisdom arises. With this wisdom, we know from all three centers, not just our heads, who we are and who we can become. Relationships provide a safe and loving container as well as providing supportive companions in the journey to our hearts. Wisdom is discovered in the arms of community, not in isolation. Being grounded in our bodies and open to our hearts allows us to remain in the present moment, knowing that what we need will arise within us—riches beyond our anticipation. In these moments, Fives know abundance and are extravagantly generous.

PRACTICES Bringing Awareness to Fives' Core Issues

Focused Inquiry

+ *When has the need to know prematurely been a barrier to your loving fully? When have you substituted information for emotion?*
+ *How do you deplete yourself?*
+ *What precipitates withdrawing for you? What allows you to stay engaged?*
+ *How do you experience your virtue of non-attachment?*

Our practices are ways of saying "yes" to our journey to our Essence.

Engagement to Counter the Type's Patterns

+ Practice saying "thank you" to increase your awareness of others' generosity.
+ At the end of each day, ask yourself, *"How was my heart affected today?"*
+ Notice when you think "I can do without that." This is retracting energy. Consider engaging in extravagance instead. Notice your body's response to this suggestion!
+ What does contraction feel like in your body? Use this sensation as an indication that you're withdrawing from connecting. Experiment with breathing through the contraction and staying engaged.
+ Remember a time when you were surprised by the generous nurturing of another. How did that feel to you? What made that possible? Daily, be generous in some way.

When authentic, Fives are connected, playful, and caring people. Privacy becomes less important as Fives nurture relationships. A grounded body brings clarity to thinking and a trust that "I am enough" and "I know enough."

BEYOND YOUR TYPE

Full knowing arises when the body is grounded, and abundance emerges in the heart that is open.

Sabbath-Keeping

Sabbath, in the traditional Jewish understanding, directs our focus to awe and provides space for us to cultivate delight in creation and our lives. Sabbath invites us to wake up to ourselves and our world.

This day's rhythm supports the emotional nurturing of Fives and allows safe space for spontaneity to occur. If possible, begin Sabbath by engaging the body in some form of movement. Stretching, yoga, exercise, or a brisk morning walk enliven the body's senses. Stay away from the computer today. Stay with your body's experience in the moment. Allow your body's instincts, rather than your mind's reason, to guide you in what comes next.

See the Sabbath as an immersion in generosity and abundance. Understand that, as Eckhart Tolle says, "Whatever you think the world is withholding from you, you are withholding from the world."[1] Contemplate those gifts and resources that you have to offer. Give something, whether it be a donation to a charity, a pot of soup to a sick neighbor, or a hug to a friend. Give. If married or partnered, don't rely on your intimate to connect you with others. Initiate a phone call or an activity with someone. At some point during the day, spend some time journaling, remembering the nurturing you received during the past week. Spend this day in a posture of thanksgiving for those who were generous.

A Type Five Prayer

Awaken in me my full knowing, that I may remember my heart's desire. Give me eyes to see the many ways that life is abundant, the many blessings offered me each day, that I may receive my heart's desire. Ground of my Being, empty me now of my need for predictability that stifles my spontaneity. Soften my withholding that I may be more generous with others. Give me the wisdom to know when to think and when to act. Calm my fears of rejection, and instill in me the courage to open my heart and share myself with others in ways that cultivate compassion. Coming into my full senses, I offer gratitude for my body's wisdom. May I begin each day, grounded in that wisdom and in my presence, knowing that I have enough—enough time, energy, information, and passion—to live fully engaged in life with others.

CHAPTER 12
The Power of Abiding: Type Seven

When most of us think about Sevens, an image of an energetic, friendly extrovert comes to mind. Yet, Sevens can be introverts as well, prompting a broader understanding of this type. Whether introverts or extroverts, all Sevens want alone time. Solitude allows Sevens space for engaging their minds, quiet time, hobbies and crafts. As you read this chapter, invite the type Seven within you to come forward.

TYPE SEVEN AT A GLANCE

Strengths: Curious, generates ideas and options, playful, integrates information quickly

Ego Ideal: I am upbeat and positive.

Focus of Attention: Best case

Motivation: To be stimulated

Worldview: The world is limiting and I might miss something.

Fixation: Planning

Vice: Gluttony

Holy Idea: Holy Work

Virtue: Constancy

Brief Overview

With a positive spirit, quick mind, and trusting nature, Sevens make interactions fun. They have a charm that puts others at ease, and their multiple interests allow Sevens to make numerous connections in conversations. Their playful and light energy can lift the tone of a room and shift the mood. Sevens' focus of attention on best-case scenarios brings options and possibilities that generate hope and enthusiasm. This helps unstick thought processes and move decisions and actions forward. Sevens are good in brainstorming sessions because of their pattern of seeking positive possibilities and ability to ideate. They're quick to spot the most interesting person in the room.

Sevens' focus on the best case and upbeat energy moves them through relational difficulties without holding grudges, a lovely component of this type structure. On the downside, this focus and energy creates a naivety that engenders a blind trust in others. When optimism is unrealistic, Sevens may follow a troublesome path that can lead to a distorted view of reality with some self-deception. This self-deception can show up as trusting someone who isn't trustworthy or not recognizing the difficulties in a given situation.

The vice of type Seven is gluttony. This isn't about food; it is a gluttony of the mind. Gluttony encourages the continuous generation of options, possibilities, and ideas. It presents a barrier to depth and focused action, causing Sevens to flit quickly from one activity or plan to the next. This vice fuels a drive to fill the mind with imaginative plans and fill calendars with new experiences. More than once on type panels or in individual sessions I've heard Sevens describe an all-pervading sense of starving, always wanting more. This sensation prompts an active seeking to fill the void with a change of scenery, a new career, a new lover. Planning the next exciting adventure is a wonderful escape route from the fear of emptiness, or having no options, that lurks beneath gluttony. When Sevens excitedly present options and possibilities, this indicates that gluttony is the master puppeteer of the moment. Sevens may want to consider, *"How does gluttony limit me?"*

Moving on to the next stimulating possibility becomes an addictive cycle that has its own limitations, one of which is missing the treasures available in the present moment. Staying steady with the familiar may feel confining, especially if there is no curiosity about what is familiar. If Sevens can explore the familiar with new eyes, with a beginner's mind, then they can become enchanted anew with their current experience.

Throughout her teaching career, Helen Palmer would often comment that when you scratch a Seven, you get a Six. Unpacking this statement, we remember that these types are in the triad whose primary emotional issue is fear, and Sevens respond to this emotion by attempting to outrun it. Staying busy and seeking stimulation keeps fear at a safe distance. When no stimuli are available, anxiety arises. While they may seem optimistic, worst-case thinking can wreak internal havoc.

When relying on their own perspective and not engaging with others, Sevens fall into projection. This is the defense mechanism of Sixes, but it plays a role in the landscape of Sevens too. With their active imaginations, Sevens may create false inner narratives that suggest a positive slant, such as "I'm okay, so you're okay too!" Usually, Sevens assume they will be welcomed and liked. They have a strong desire for others to mirror their positivity and enthusiasm. "Yes, that's a great idea!" is an example of positive mirroring. If this kind of mirroring doesn't occur, Sevens may look to someone else until they find it.

On the other hand, the Seven's imagination might conjure up a narrative suggesting that another is judging them in harsh ways. When their false inner narratives take a downward turn, Sevens can become highly critical of themselves or others. This behind-the-scenes view of Sevens as critical and fearful is one that is rarely seen by others. Yet, being aware of this part of their inner landscape brings to light a **compassionate entry point** for those who know and love people who lead with this type. When in low moods, at times created by their internal critic, Sevens will detach and seek private time. This is an often-used strategy by Sevens to hide their sadness, as they fear being a downer to others. This, too, is a projection. Knowing that others' low moods can bring them down, Sevens project that others feel the same way. Not true! Reminding Sevens that all of who they are is welcomed is an act of kindness. Actually, Sevens can seem more real to us when they share their low moments, fears, and sorrows.

When living on automatic, the gnawing question for this type is, *"What am I missing that will make me complete?"* Sevens may consider asking themselves, *"How does this moment offer me completeness? Who am I when I'm not seeking stimulation?"*

The Striving and the Avoidance

Sevens are naturally curious about learning and enthusiastically welcome new experiences, new adventures, and meeting new people. They find excitement in the unexplored. The husband of a friend who leads with Seven recently told their daughter, "Your mother is prone to enthusiasms!" Sevens can seem fearless, with an attitude of "Life is to be lived and experienced. Let's go!" A deep fear of missing out drives the striving to experience more, and then more. The next new experience may be just what was missing!

To prevent themselves from missing out, Sevens are on the look-out for limitations, which can be real or imagined. They tend to see limits where none exist, and efforts to avoid them can be obvious or subtle. While Sevens love making plans, they commonly deviate from those plans, since plans can feel limiting. Sevens prize freedom. They want things to happen on their timeline, and while their ever-changing agendas may give them the appearance of flexibility,

Sevens are actually quite inflexible. I learned this years ago when facilitating a type Seven group. I invited the group to engage in an exercise: at least three times in the next week, follow someone else's agenda. Then, notice what thoughts and sensations come up for you as you go along with that person's plans. The moans and resistance to the idea were comical, and we all had a good laugh. In the group meeting that followed this exercise, the Sevens reported how difficult they'd found it to go along with another's plan. In the midst of it, their minds indicated the numerous ways that they would have done things differently, and better! From this exercise, we all learned about Sevens' need to control their own lives.

The defense mechanism for this type is rationalization, or reframing to the positive. When obstacles or difficulties arise, Sevens look for the silver lining or the opportunity. This has various effects. At times, a positive spin brings hope or inspiration to keep going. Other times, the reframing is a form of deflecting, shifting Sevens away from feelings and into the head to intellectualize the situation. Rationalization may lessen emotional pain in the moment, but it creates distance and disconnection from oneself and from others. An appropriate inquiry for Sevens regarding rationalizing might be, *"Is my positive reframing arising from a sense of hope or a need to avoid?"*

The Core Fear and the Pivot

Sevens unconsciously believe that the world is limiting, confining them in ways that deprive them of new experiences. Yet, tasting the new and moving on to the next shiny enticement eventually proves to be wearing, and within the unconsciousness of Sevens is a desire for limits, for a tether. Something within seeks a container that offers a sure-footedness, a presence that is restful. Sevens have an underlying false belief that without the external stimulation that "the new" offers, they will tumble into a pit of emptiness or emotional pain. Here lies the core fear: sadness is an empty, bottomless dark hole that is inescapable. The longer Sevens avoid emotional pain, the larger it seems. Fear grows. Accompanying our beloved Sevens in the pain, without judgment, is a **compassionate entry point** that can allow them to feel it more deeply and to stay with it a little longer, allowing the pain to simply be.

When staying with and moving through their emotional pain, Sevens offer themselves the gift of an abiding presence. This is the virtue of constancy. They don't abandon the truth of themselves for an adventure, but stay with what is true in the moment, without fear, and feel into the emotions and sensations that are arising. Sorrow is an experience to be felt and explored with curiosity. The holy virtue of constancy arises when Sevens stay steady in those times when stimulation is lacking and emotional pain may be emerging. Constancy brings a sense of depth and completeness. This virtue creates a spaciousness that welcomes all, be it joy, emotional pain, or sorrow. In experiencing sorrow's depths, Sevens open themselves to experiencing the depths of joy as well. Their excitability recedes as constancy becomes a source of calm that plants the seeds for joy.

Sevens: *The present moment offers the richness and joy you seek. Open yourself to it!*

Companion Voices

As you read the stories from the companion writers, be open to finding a part of you in their shared experiences.

Choosing depth rather than moving into options is important work for Sevens. Our next contributor, **Zoë**, describes the necessary inner work of allowing and feeling emotions rather than running from them. "Abiding with self" is necessary in order to "abide with others."

Giselle Buchanan once said, "It's never too late to reacquaint yourself with the forgotten parts you set aside in order to survive in a difficult world."

This quote speaks to me and the inner work I'm doing of diving into deep places in community with others. I participated in the Enneagram Prison Project and took part in their guide training program. I didn't realize that learning about the Enneagram would feel like being thrown off a dock into water. There is no going back to a state of less presence or depth. Working with the Enneagram has been transformational, painful, and freeing. One of my desires in working with my type Seven is to feel safe enough with myself and others to share freely. Key work is learning how to be with my grief without letting it swallow me whole. Through my Enneagram work, I've learned that an illusion of type Seven is that grief is a bottomless pit. Over time, I began distancing myself from that illusion. Now, I'm feeling safe enough to allow grief to wash over me, whether in powerful waves or small licks, and honor it as my teacher. This allowing brings the gift of greater depth.

My name is Zoë. I'm nonbinary and use they/them and he/him pronouns. Working with my type and going deep into myself and my experiences was intense and necessary for me to open my heart, still my mind, and be in my body. I was able to hold and nurture parts of myself that had needed holding my whole life. For example, when I am not present to myself, the energy I expend to "fake" the image of someone who is upbeat and positive is actually more chaotic and damaging than my fear of losing control, or expressing my sadness, or experiencing the unknown. Maintaining this upbeat image ignores any sad emotions. This habit keeps me imprisoned, distancing me from my authentic self.

When I experienced my first period as a young person, my mom celebrated the occasion by taking me out to buy a book and enjoy a sauna together. She said something like "This means you're a woman now," and it was like a part of me crumpled. I couldn't get the words out, but inside me I was shouting: "But I don't want to be!" I felt sad, but unable to explore my feelings around this experience. My constricting did not allow me to identify or explore what was causing my sadness. As I write this, my throat tightens just as it did years ago when I struggled to express my trapped feelings to my mom.

Lots of feelings were left behind and trapped as some part of me guided me away from what didn't feel good. My ego directed me to fake a state of "I'm okay," which feels safe, but is not safe or freeing. While I recognize this was perhaps intelligent to survive as a child, it no longer serves me. To deny my fear of being in pain or sad to keep others happy is no longer what I want in my life. Staying on the bright side of life avoids true depth of connection. In my younger years, the Seven's defense mechanism of rationalization "protected" me from confronting and engaging difficulties. A part of me needed this protection. This constant positive reframing isn't as helpful now.

A hard part about being nonbinary is running into assumptions people make about me and the innocent ignorance of an incredibly binary world. Growing up, I didn't have trans or nonbinary elders in my life, nor did I have queer elders. In our heterosexual-dominant world, the expression of queer and trans voices is often relegated to hidden corners. And it took me 20 years of life to realize there were more options than the limited and binary gender identities I had known up until that point.

These days, my type Seven virtue of constancy, staying with what's arising and dropping into feelings, is a way of honoring myself. I advocate for and honor myself by being with both joy and sadness. I allow people to join and support me and be companions in the harder stuff, as we all share in the human experience of contradictions wrapped in a full range of emotions. Finding compassion for myself and for others in community is key as I continue my inner work.

Honoring all experiences and emotions is the path toward freedom and joy for Zoë. As a nonbinary person, they continue to work to be authentic, drawing on their inner courage. The Seven's ego ideal of being upbeat and positive is a strong barrier to recognizing and sharing their sadness and fear with others. Yet, when Sevens can muster the courage to do this, as Zoë has, they become familiar with some of the positive aspects of sadness and receive the compassion of community.

Ann, our next contributor, demonstrates steadiness in the face of struggles. The daily container of a structure of care for her spouse brings her into the freedom of each present moment.

I am a Southern Jewish woman born into an interfaith family that struggled with alcoholism. I sought comfort in friendships and adoring grandmothers to soothe hidden wounds. Career choices reflected my need to search for a life beyond the routine and create meaningful experiences for myself and for others. My life choices were often in sync with my quest for variety, challenges, start-ups, and success in my pursuits.

I left New Orleans for college in Denver, a city and school I had never visited and where I knew very few people. I jumped into a 1968 world far from my private school coddling and explored unfamiliar arenas. The traditional route in graduate school laid the path for me to pursue a challenging career at our local zoo and create programs that were unmatched in their impact on visitors. Interesting and apropos for me and my optimistic Seven self, the staff named these "Camelot Years" at Audubon. The zoo was a breeding ground for young innovators, and we eagerly grew programs, built education buildings, and recruited countless volunteers of all ages. I rose in the ranks and led a talented team, proud of our contributions. Each day was varied, fast paced, and pursued a conservationists' vision.

In my work, I traveled extensively as the education department I directed partnered with zoos and aquariums across the country. I loved exploring new relationships and expanding opportunities. At times, I may have been ill prepared as I was thrown into unfamiliar territory—but it would have gone against my every belief to demonstrate lack of skill or preparation.

As one who leads with Seven, my days begin with optimism, enthusiasm, and a zest for life, eager to greet new horizons. However, difficulties throughout my life have opened me to more than the positive aspects of life. In retrospect, I realize that I created an armor to protect myself, believing that I, alone, could protect myself from deep wounds. I valued self-reliance, strength, ingenuity, and resiliency. When I needed a job to support myself and my children following my divorce, I found three and worked seven days a week. I counted on my instincts and had great confidence in myself. Everything seemed "figure-out-able," and I plunged ahead.

Cracks began to surface as my first marriage crumbled and I chose to leave. I mourned the visible pain inflicted on my children. I sought the solace of solid friendships and the wisdom of a therapist. Seldom had I allowed another to see the cracks in my armor, as we Sevens prefer private detachment. Yet, with this support, I prepared for the next phase of my life, a challenging and rewarding professional life as well my second marriage, to my husband Larry. Life was a whirlwind, and I found comfort in the harried life balancing four children with busy school schedules, a beloved husband, friends, and a much-loved career. There are many books written about blended families, and we felt like we were writing an original version . . . there was no option but success. And then . . .

In 2005, Katrina tore my city of New Orleans and my home apart. I muddled through a few years alone, among a city of "the wounded." Again, individual therapy supported my healing and growth. I threw myself into an unknown arena again, volunteering for a civic organization that sought to rebuild a broken criminal justice system. Not my area of expertise, far from the zoo world, but I understood consensus building and creating programs that serve diverse and critical needs. I remained at the table until legislation and programs were created.

And then, still raw from the pain of Katrina, I received news that dropped me to my knees. My husband Larry was diagnosed with a debilitating, degenerative muscle disease with no known cure or treatment.

Gratefully, my husband and I are both fighters. We moved forward, researched, sought the advice of expert medical professionals, and adapted with each progression of his disease. I was a believer in hope through action. Surrender was never an option. Hurdles were high, but tackled with determination and lots of love and support. All seemed doable as we fought the invisible enemy that took a very visible toll. I leaned on my creativity and ingenuity, and we leaned on each other to build a life able to accommodate an ever-evolving illness. I trusted my ability to tirelessly persevere amidst the unknown.

Yet, the tasks I was undertaking to fight for Larry's survival didn't allow me to see myself clearly. My head prevailed while my heart began to wrap up tightly again. I did not allow myself to feel disappointment. My problem-solving mind stepped up, a gift and a curse. Making decisions and solving problems creates an illusion that uncertainty no longer exists, and the impermanence of life gets lost in busyness. As I remained fixed in my head, my heart was breaking. When do I surrender to the reality of loss? Seldom do I stop to consider that and other questions about Larry's life and death.

To return to my heart, I seek the quiet and beauty of the outdoors. My small walled garden provides the peace I need to renew. Walking with my beloved rescue retriever is a necessary part of my day. Friendships are paring down to a trusted few with whom I feel safe to uncover my wounded heart. I welcome the quiet to allow the pain in my heart to emerge, my faith to grow, and my courage and resiliency to be sustained. Enneagram teachings encourage my opening to the many facets of myself, becoming more curious about myself and learning what constancy, the virtue of Sevens, feels like. I am learning that I can be grateful and mourn simultaneously. I can hold both sorrow and joy in my open heart.

I am learning to love in the moment, and when I do, my love deepens. There is a *freedom* in not knowing what lies ahead. Life's gift is the present time with my beloved Larry, living one step at a time. This "staying with" brings me such fullness. A key practice for me is to allow the fears of tomorrow to surface, notice and allow them, then return to the present.

Taking one step at a time, I can see how the challenges and gifts of my life have opened me to better understand others' pain and to grow compassion within me. Sometimes I still struggle not to be dismissive of another's emotional or physical pain. But healing myself allows me to nurture my compassionate self. I have faced joys and hardships in my life, experienced both exhaustion and exhilaration. Along the way, I've learned to trust and to journey at the pace of my loved ones, knowing all I have is today. It is enough.

There is something about deep wounding that can be a pathway to deep, deep love. It's a very beautiful thing when the wound becomes the doorway.

—HENRY SHUKMAN[1]

Love is a powerful motivator to shift patterns, and Ann embodies constancy in her love for her spouse. She abides. She creates a rhythm in her own self-care and in the care of her husband, a rhythm that creates a container in which she drops deeper, to know the depth of love. Without wanting or needing to know ahead of time, the planning mind stills. She stays in the present moment and knows the freedom it offers.

Alchemy: From Type to Essence

Holy Work as Enlightened Spiritual Perspective

Years ago, I watched a 2008 documentary, *Man on Wire*, about a Frenchman who strung a wire between New York's World Trade Center towers (when they existed) and, without a safety net and high above the city, walked on this wire from one tower to the next. This walk required a focused presence. Indeed, his life depended on his focus and presence. For me, this was a demonstration of the powerful presence that Sevens are capable of. All types, when we receive our Holy Idea or enlightened spiritual perspective, embody that perspective. Sevens embody presence.

Holy Work, the enlightened spiritual perspective of the Seven, is the work of being present in this moment and allowing presence to arise. In presence, Sevens' planning ceases and they allow the universal flow to unfold. They trust something beyond their own agenda. Fears of limitations, emptiness, and emotional pain dissolve, making the heart accessible. Reverence is the heart's offspring. It creates spaciousness for an "I/thou" relationship. Reverence deepens us all to the unfolding of the moment, empties us of everything but "now" so that we may know the sacredness of our lives. A rich abiding with ourselves, moment by moment, reminds us that we are whole.

Who we are awaits us, beyond that which we use to fill ourselves. In emptiness, we discover that we are complete. We are enough.

PRACTICES Bringing Awareness to Sevens' Core Issues

Focused Inquiry

+ *When has your curiosity disconnected you from relating? How does your body give you clues that you've disconnected?*
+ *When have you felt complete and filled by deepening a commitment?*
+ *How might your sadness be a gateway to your loving fully? What are the positive aspects of sadness?*
+ *Is emptiness scary for you? If so, why is this? What color or shape is emptiness?*
+ *How do you discern the difference between gluttony and action? Consider your body's posture and pace in each.*

Our practices are ways of saying "yes" to our journey to our Essence.

Engagement to Counter the Type's Patterns

+ When you notice your mind moving into future plans, ask yourself, *"Is my planning connected to or separate from what is occurring in this moment?"*
+ When you experience grief or sadness, allow yourself time with it. When you feel ready to move on, stay with the sadness for two more minutes.
+ Notice when a "move on" energy is activated in you, and bring your body's energy to your midsection. Breathe into the belly and acknowledge your emotional state.

- Once each week, practice following someone else's agenda. Notice what thoughts and sensations arise as you engage with their plan.
- How does your sensitivity to being seen as incompetent drive your projections? Notice when this occurs, and check out your inner narratives (projections) with others.

A constant seeking of the new arises from the need for external stimulation. When Sevens discover the fascinating adventures of the inner life, reverence becomes a companion. A quiet heart emerges that deepens the experience of the present moment.

BEYOND YOUR TYPE

A grounded presence resides within and allows you to draw from the deep wells of both your joy and your sadness.

Sabbath-Keeping

Sabbath, in the traditional Jewish understanding, directs our focus to awe and provides space for us to cultivate delight in creation and our lives. Sabbath invites us to wake up to ourselves and our world.

Sabbath day for Sevens is a day to cultivate a quiet heart that brings forth reverence. Reverence requires paying attention and taking in what is before us, being mindful of where we are in space and time, to whom and what we are relating. It allows and honors what is and brings about a heart connection. No investigation with the mind. No imagining, no planning.

To guide Sevens on their inner journey, this day is structured to soak in the present moment. There is nothing on the calendar today. The day is free of agenda. Multitasking is set aside for the pleasure of experiencing one thing at a time. Practice completing one thing before moving to the next. Ground your joy in the moment with a single focus of attention. Engage your body in slow, deliberate movements. Pause when you notice your mind spinning out to future possibilities and plans, and reconnect with what is taking place in the moment. Return to your body's sensations. Land in your body's experience of the present moment. If you spend time with another, offer space for deeper conversation that allows you to connect from your heart. Consider the difference between an open heart and a connected heart. *Where does mutuality exist in your life?*

A Type Seven Prayer

Ground of my Being, you offer the completion I seek. Gently guide me to the fulfillment that is awaiting me when I rest in the calm of the present moment. Ease my planning mind and the ideas that overwhelm me. May my energy deepen rather than scatter me, so that I experience the gifts each moment offers that lead me to my wholeness. May I attune to my heart so that I feel my joy, and also the richness of my sadness. Both bring me home to my deeper Self, where I find the freedom to be me. Guide me on the path toward reverence, for in that moment, I know that love has no limits. In the present moment, I discover that I am missing nothing. The present moment offers a limitless abundance of wonder and awe.

PART THREE

Resistance and Receptivity

CHAPTER 13
Resistance and Receptivity

Awareness is our natural state, but we don't recognize it. A receptive heart re-sides in us always, yet our focus of attention, emotional habit, and motivations keep us in the play of our personality type. Movement toward ease is the process of spiritual transformation. It is the movement toward receptivity that allows spiritual experience to arise. Type can't have a spiritual experience.

—HELEN PALMER, author, co-founder of the Narrative Enneagram Tradition, lectures and meditations

For most of my life, the natural world has been one of my greatest teachers. Living in a location with four distinct seasons reminds me of the cycles of life. Birth, life, death, all a part of the whole. Gardeners know this rhythm in the planting, tending, and harvesting process. The Solstice and Equinox are moments to acknowledge the passing of time and to ask, *"What within me is longing to be birthed or to be heard or seen? What within me is growing stronger? What have I outgrown that is ready to be released?"* We humans are ever changing, and these questions are appropriate in any season of our lives.

It seems to me that we, as a part of the natural world, live in a spiral of cycles rather than linear time. I have tested this belief time and again when I feel overwhelmed by too many tasks coming my way. When I begin to feel anxious, I sit still for three minutes, drink in the quiet, and breathe. Each time I engage in this practice, it seems that more time becomes available when I return to my tasks. All gets done with time to spare. I am amazed by the elasticity of time. If we understood time as abundant rather than scarce and slipping through our fingers, would we slow our pace?

In her lectures and writing, the late author and anthropologist Angeles Arrien taught that the pace of the natural world is "medium to slow." When we pay attention and become more present, this pace holds us as we walk forest trails, climb mountains, wander in the desert, and kayak rivers. Humans turn to the natural world for solace, for hope, for grounding. Because we are a part of the natural world, something within us desires a slower pace. We miss ourselves in our hurried lives. We outrun our hearts and neglect our fragility when we move fast. In the larger context of creation, we know that we are a part of the whole, the great All. It's why we go outside to engage in vision quests. In solitude, with the natural world and without agenda, we gain clarity as we return to being present with ourselves. Visions simply come as we attune to ourselves and relax into the embrace of our natural surroundings. Our inner spaciousness grows in this holding. Right here, right now is a most miraculous space.

The natural world has a rich "is-ness." It speaks in present tense: "I am." The rooted ones—plants, grasses, trees—remind us to be who we are. Held in the gentle fierceness of the natural world, we can relax into our wholeness. Can we imagine a flower striving to bloom? Of course not! Flowers bloom when plants receive sunlight, rain, and air, with soil as a container. Life wants to live. Aliveness abounds in the is-ness of nature without effort. In this oneness, there is nothing to prove, nothing to defend. Life flows naturally, allowing and receiving. Trees shed leaves then receive buds of new life, all unfolding in life's sacred rhythms.

Allowing and receiving can be foreign to humans. Unlike plants and trees, we may lack trust in our unfolding. So, we intervene and direct, manipulate and question. We hesitate or rush headstrong into whatever is next. We strive. We resist. Pulling back and pushing forward are both forms of resistance. We resist more often than we realize; it is a part of our automatic patterns.

Striving resists what *is*. It denies our experience of the moment. We miss the morning's birdsong, the dog's longing gaze, the possibility of deepening our relationships with ourselves and others. What does this resistance feel like in the body? Regardless of the focus of our resistance, our body's patterns of resisting will be similar each time. A contracted body is a clue that resistance is in operation. We contract, and other sensations follow. Are we guarded, or open to our hearts? Where is the breath in our body? What is our current emotional state? Being curious about what we are experiencing in the moment can open us to see more clearly the patterns that hold us captive and maintain our posture of resistance.

The chapters in Part Two provided a brief discussion of each of the nine types' particular form of striving. Whether striving to fill a void with new experiences (Sevens), to be different (Fours), or to maintain harmony (Nines), we believe that our desire for stimulation (Sevens), or to be seen (Fours), or for peace (Nines) will be fulfilled by our attempts to secure what we think we need. We can remember countless times when our efforts brought the desired results, so we continue in these patterns. Our aspirations to be seen, to be secure and safe, and to be treated fairly are respectable and seem necessary to us. Depending on our life experiences, ethnicity, and culture, these goals may seem attainable or may feel beyond reach. Our type's striving shapes our posture and sets our pace as we work toward fulfilling our current purpose. Our bodies know the rhythm and hold on to the pattern of this striving energy.

The more we strive, the more we distance ourselves from our Holy Idea, from our Essence, our deeper compassionate Self. Striving resists the natural flow and rhythms of our lives, creates imbalance, and is exhausting. Perhaps it takes exhaustion for us to realize that something is amiss and that we can choose another path. I am reminded of the Tagore quote I offered earlier in the book: "Everything comes to us that belongs to us if we create the capacity to receive it." How do we cultivate this capacity to receive?

Receiving is scary for us all. We may feel unprepared, out of control, uncertain, vulnerable. To receive is to allow the next without knowledge of the outcome. Can we trust ourselves enough to relax into receptivity? This is a difficult choice point for us. We can be moved by fear and perpetuate our striving, or we can pause, take three breaths, ground ourselves, and trust ourselves. When we move into a receptive posture, *we receive reality rather than perceiving reality through the lens of our type.* In this expansive, receptive posture (our enlightened spiritual perspective), we know the Oneness to which we belong. What seemed so frightening suddenly is not. A Hebrew proverb states, "Change happens in an instant. It's resisting that takes a lifetime." We change moment by moment, bit by bit, drawing on our courage and inner strength. Allowing brings a fullness to our living. When the energy of striving arises, if we can engage in a three-breath pause, ground ourselves, and relax into allowing, into receptivity, then we wake up. In wakefulness we are aware of being carried.

No doubt, this is easier said than done. But with awareness and practice, we can create choice points. Automatic patterns or new pathways? The gift of the Enneagram is a map of our egoic patterns. This map allows us to observe those patterns and recognize when they are operating more clearly and more quickly. Knowing what is driving us makes choice possible. In this moment, we can choose the comfort of familiar patterns, or we can choose to become more than we believe ourselves to be.

These questions can support us in our becoming:

+ *What supports you in noticing your type's automatic patterns and arriving at a choice point?*
+ *What resources do you lean into in order to move through your fear?*

May our responses bring forth a deeper self-understanding.

Vice to Virtue Alchemy

Striving energy constricts us and indicates that we may be in the grip of our type's vice. Shifting from the energy of our vice to the energy of our virtue is significant work that first requires catching the vice in the moment. Knowing how our vice operates is an important part of this work. The vice is the fuel that powers the small story of ourselves, the ego ideal. It is a core part of our suffering. Self-observation, noticing our sensations and our focus of attention, is key for discerning the ways our vice moves us and engages us in automatic patterns. A noticeable first clue is a contracted body. How does your vice feel in your body? Like molasses, if you lead with Nine? Like a powerful force arising if you lead with Eight? Sevens may feel excited when gluttony arises. What's it like for you?

Once we realize that we are contracted and operating from our vice, we can choose to continue on automatic, or choose to wake up. Remembering that the vice is energy—that it's fluid, no matter how solid and strong it feels—can help us sustain our curiosity.

The practice of shifting energy begins with *noticing* the vice is operating. Then we *pause*; we sense down into our feet, *ground* ourselves in our bodies, and bring awareness to the vice energy that wants to move us in the usual way. However, getting present and focusing on the sensations of our vice is not business as usual! Usually, we remain unaware or don't notice and move along as best we can. Staying with the *felt sense* of the vice energy helps us shift our focus from the thoughts and stories in our minds and remain with our bodies. How would you describe the sensations of your vice? Be curious about those sensations as you observe them without judgment. Welcome them, and allow the energy to be as big as it wants to be. Welcome with curiosity while not expressing the energy. Abide with this constricted energy; allow it, be curious about the energy. See your vice as fluid energy that responds to your awareness. A steady focus on the sensations of vice energy supports the energy in shifting toward expansion and compassion. With practice, this shifting will take less time. *Alchemy, the shift, happens in the allowing, the welcoming of what is.* Historically, alchemy is the transformation of base metal into gold. Here, alchemy within us allows the beauty of who we are to come forward, converting our vice energy to our virtue energy. Allowing creates inner spaciousness.

Using type Nine as an example, Nines might notice the pullback energy of lethargy—a sense of heaviness and indifference. Upon noticing this, Nines can pause and breathe, and focus on the energy of lethargy without acting on or expressing that energy. This means, for Nines, not withdrawing. The next step is getting curious and allowing this vice to become as large as it wants, with no judgment. Staying curious about the vice is, in itself, an act of self-remembering.

As Nines engage in a steady focus on the sensation of lethargy, it begins to shift. They may observe the mind's fogginess clearing. The body may seem lighter. Eventually, a sense of aliveness emerges that supports Nines in showing up and valuing themselves. In this clarity, there is no duality of "my agenda" or "your agenda." What comes forward is a both/and understanding that supports all of us showing up.

Don't fight it, invite it!

The *Tao Te Ching* says, "If you want to shrink something, you must first allow it to expand. If you want to get rid of something, you must first allow it to flourish."[1]

When working to transform energy, whether it's the vice or a stuck emotion, the body will save us! Some years ago, when I was first getting a clue that my body is my container for alchemy—for transforming energy—I created the PAUSE Process, described in the following section.[2] This process of separating the emotion from the story about the emotion is useful when an emotion is ruling us for a lengthy time period.

When we deflect, suppress, or even express an emotion, we aren't *feeling* the emotion. Telling someone how angry I am and why I'm angry doesn't dissolve the anger. In fact, talking about it can exacerbate the anger. Thinking about the emotion and creating strategies for tamping it down or avoiding it are forms of spiritual bypass. We bypass when we observe an emotion but don't feel it, when we consider the "why" of our emotions and analyze them without engaging them. Avoiding and refusing to engage with an emotion or a memory that seems intolerable to us is a spiritual bypass that keeps us in the head, distant from our body's and heart's experiences of our lives.

Patience with this process is important in the initial experiences of working with energy. The ego doesn't want to surrender the story about the emotion! Our work is to steady our focus on the felt sense of the emotion until that emotion transforms.

The PAUSE Process

Because we are inherently compassionate beings, our bodies will help us shift to compassion if we can maintain a steady attention on the state of the emotion rather than the story. The body is a powerful guide in the PAUSE Process as it anchors us in the present.

If, during this process, your mind engages with a story and takes you out of the felt sense of the emotion, simply shake off the story and begin the process again. The PAUSE Process has five steps:

P *Plant* yourself in your body, find your feet, and breathe. Be present.

A *Allow* the emotion that is arising without judging it, deflecting, or expressing it. Simply honor and allow and notice where the emotion is in your body. Be curious about it.

U *Understand* through curiosity. Am I feeling the emotion I think I'm feeling? Is there an emotion behind the presenting emotion? Ask your body. I might ask, "Am I feeling anger?" My body may respond with, "Hurt." The body's response is quick, simple, and without emotion. Now, I work with hurt rather than anger.

S *Sense* your body. Stabilize your attention on the felt sense of the emotion and let go of the internal story, the *why* of the emotion. To stay with the sensation of the emotion, ask yourself: *"What is the texture of this emotion? What is its weight? What color is it? Where is it located in my body? What are its boundaries?"* Be curious and without judgment. Continue to focus on the emotion as it begins to shift. Notice how the texture, color, and boundaries change. These questions support us in staying with the felt sense.

E *Engage* your self with the compassion that emerges from the deepest part of who you are. This compassion will naturally arise as you focus on the felt sense of the emotion.

The familiar adage "What we resist, persists" is applicable to this work. Allowing creates pathways leading to growth, and staying with an emotion or our vice without judgment or expressing it, can bring us into a quality of our Essence.

Bedrock

We all have a foundation—a ground within—that we can draw from, stand on, and turn to as a resource when we feel lost, doubt ourselves, or are in a difficult situation. When you find yourself in these moments, what tethers you? Can you describe your inner ground? What is your bedrock? What do you know to be true? When we know our bedrock, we realize that we can count on ourselves. Self-trust arises, no matter the external conditions.

Often in workshops, I'll create space for participants to reflect on their bedrock. In considering my own bedrock, I name silence as a creative partner, my faithfulness to beauty, the wisdom of trees when I invite it and listen. I believe in my inherent goodness and in the unending presence of love and abundance. When I'm lost to myself, I turn to this knowing, this bedrock, to return me to myself.

We access this foundation within ourselves when we are present. From this place, we can see ourselves through the gaze of our hearts rather than through the eyes of others. From our bedrock, we find our voice and our agency. Here we find our fullness and freedom, our wholeness. From our bedrock, presence arises and our Essence becomes who we are.

Beyond Our Type

We are more than we believe ourselves to be. With the guidance of the Enneagram Map, we see how we fall asleep to our egoic patterns, how we move in lockstep with the small story of ourselves that our ego/type structure constantly whispers to us. These patterns and stories are familiar and comfortable, so why change?

This is the central question, isn't it? How much desire do we have to engage in our inner work, to feel and move through the pain that arises when we begin to understand what living on automatic has cost us? A journaling question may be helpful: What do you sacrifice for the sake of continuing with your automatic patterns? Can we remain steadfast in this exploration even when we become discouraged, with our ego telling us we just aren't growing? These inner narratives that work to keep us small can be extraordinarily harsh. Our inner voice might say, *"What's the use? This is a waste of time!"* or even *"You aren't worth the effort."* Fear is a major tool of our ego/type structure. In choosing to be moved by fear, we live out our lives without experiencing the fullness of ourselves in our brief time in this Earth School.

Yes, we can remain steadfast to our growth. Loving ourselves and knowing our worth supports our steadfastness to be alive to our lives. Though we may sometimes take "two steps forward, one step back," along the path we glimpse and experience the joy of our wholeness as our Essence arises. We know moments when we become a manifestation of patience, compassion, and kindness. Compassion resides in our marrow. Radiance is who we are, not our type.

With this awareness of our Essence, we can engage in practices and inquiry that will transform us from our automatic self into a present and radiant self. Our Essential Self is cheering us on as we learn to relax into presence and allow what is arising without needing to control it.

This book began with a discussion of presence and returns to presence as the foundation for this alchemy to occur. As we live more in presence, our personal consciousness grows. The Enneagram

Map lights the way to our deeper selves, naming our virtue and our enlightened spiritual perspective. Old patterns and false narratives continue their journey with us, but with more awareness of them, we need not believe them or act on them. We have the power of choice, and we have our Essence that is always nudging us and inviting us to allow its arising.

The healing of ourselves and the world depends on this allowing, this waking up to the goodness and love within us. I believe that our greatest work is waking up to ourselves. Living in wakefulness, we know that love precedes, follows, and abides with us. We need only open to it and receive. This poem by Rumi captures the essence of this understanding:

> *When I run after what I think I want, my days are a furnace of stress and anxiety; if I sit in my own place of patience, what I need flows to me, and without pain. From this, I understand that what I want also wants me, is looking for me and attracting me. There is a great secret here for anyone who can grasp it.*[3]

Blessings for the Nine Types

In conclusion, I'd like to offer the following blessings for the nine types:

Nines: There is something creative and impactful emerging in you. From this place, you are confident and you will not be overwhelmed. An *Alive Heart* chooses your own desires and claims you! In aliveness, both/and thinking is possible. Your agenda and the other's agenda emerge with ease, without disharmony. The Alive Heart brings your authentic love forward, and you teach us Divine Union.

Eights: There is something fragile and open gently rising in you. A *Tender Heart* allows others to impact you with their kindness and love. Mutuality is a given as you receive the care of others. All are for you. There are no dualities. From this place, you know unity. We are one. Your armor softens/fades the more your heart opens. Kindness flows from your tender strength.

Ones: There is something forgiving and expansive breaking ground in you. A *Gracious Heart* opens you to feeling the goodness in yourself. Now, acceptance of all of who you are comes naturally. Grace requires nothing from you. From here, you enter the lightness of flawed perfection and offer your nonjudging presence to the world. Peace radiates from within you and beyond.

Threes: There is something loving and patient being birthed in you, inviting you to trust that you are not alone in the doing. Moving at a slower pace, you know that your being is lovable. Doing matters not. Your *Authentic Heart* emerges. Now you accept all of you and know that your being and presence are impressive enough. You live from your depths. Your capacity for relating deepens, and you receive the love that has been there for you all along—without the performance.

Twos: There is something courageous and receptive beckoning you, inviting you into a genuine relationship with yourself. A balanced life of giving and receiving is possible from this place of self-approval. A *Receptive Heart* emerges, with the courage to receive and to allow life to unfold without an agenda. You can trust that connections are there, even in your solitude. From here, your sense of worth is strong, and you can rest in that knowing.

Fours: There is something steady and light growing in you that awakens you to the beauty and depth that is here now. There is no need to create it through emotion. The genuine self is birthed in the *Grateful Heart*. What you are seeking is who you already are, whole with nothing missing. Go forth and offer your deep calm to yourself and the world.

Sixes: There is something courageous and endless arising in you. In your solidness, the "what ifs" hold no power. Doubt dissolves and fear gives rise to faith. A *Courageous Heart* understands that fear is an invitation to go more deeply into what is here now. Courage supports looking within, knowing there is bedrock, a steadfastness within yourself that you can trust and draw from. From here, you are trusting and trustworthy. You come alive in the uncertain and know that you can count on yourself.

Fives: There is something overflowing and infinite arising in you. From here, your depletion is an illusion. You know in your marrow that you have more than enough. When present, clarity comes and the truth of reality is revealed. Insight comes without effort or trying to figure it out. A *Generous Heart* that connects and engages fully emerges. Go forth as abundance leads you into an openhanded response to life.

Sevens: There is something reverent and deep breaking ground in you, allowing you to be present to yourself with the capacity to savor the moment. Joy arises from a *Quiet Heart* (not scattered excitement). A Quiet Heart is expansive, soothing the grasping of gluttony. In this moment, you know that you are missing nothing. From this place, you move in grounded joy and reverence arises as you know, in the core of you, the sacredness of life.

In the choreography of your life yet to come,
May your giving and receiving be balanced,
May a song of delight sing daily in your heart's depths,
May you know the world as a generous and abundant place,
May love guide you more than fear.

May love be our legacy.

Companion Voice Biographies

This book would not exist without the contributions from these writers (listed here in order of appearance in the book). Thank you!

For type Nine:

Rev. Claire Helton is a hospice chaplain in Pensacola, FL. She previously served as a pastor in churches in Louisiana and Texas within the progressive Alliance of Baptists. Claire and her clergy spouse, Zach, are particularly grateful for the Enneagram's wisdom as they raise their two boys. She looks forward to the many days of mindful Ennea-parenting ahead.

Dr. Theresa Pavin Steward is a performing and creative artist and musicologist based in Richmond, VA, who currently works as pianist/organist and church administrator at Grace Baptist Church of Richmond. With degrees from the University of Virginia and the University of Edinburgh (UK), her research and publications have focused on Iranian popular music studies, but more recently she finds herself writing about her spiritual journey as a Muslim working in a Baptist church. Her passions are many, but mostly she aims to create a greater awareness of global music cultures through her musicological work, and she strives to craft powerful and prayerful moments of joy and gratitude, peace and reflection, through music performance and visual art.

For type Eight:

Satoya Foster, MMin, is a multi-passionate creative who explores the intersections of art and intentional living. With a deep appreciation for the beauty and meaning in everyday moments, she infuses her work and words with a sense of purpose and authenticity. As a nonprofit leader, educator, and instructional designer, Satoya has skillfully woven her passions together, empowering others to connect with themselves and live authentically. With expertise as a trauma recovery coach, professional vocalist and recording artist, and licensed cosmetologist, Satoya brings a unique perspective to her work.

Satoya received her Master of Ministry degree from Richmont Graduate University in the Mission School of Ministry cohort. She is certified in nonprofit management through Duke University. Satoya is trained in diversity, equity, inclusion, and belonging through the University of Minnesota. She is a Certified Trauma Recovery Coach through the International Association of Trauma Recovery Coaches. You can connect with Satoya at www.satoyafoster.com.

Lee Ensign is a clinical psychologist in private practice. She is a certified teacher of the Enneagram and works with interface of psychological, somatic, and spiritual experience. She lives in Knoxville, TN, and is the mother of two adult daughters.

Laurel Ensign Simmons is a mental and behavioral health professional working with children and adolescents. She is currently living in Knoxville, TN. She is joyously her mother's daughter.

For type One:

Frederica Helmiere is an explorer of tools available to respond to civilizational crises, especially the modern West's loss of the sacred.

For 20 years she has been playing at the intersections of ecology, spirituality, and social justice, as a student, researcher, professor, global professional, nonprofit leader, and backcountry enthusiast. She has master's degrees from Yale Divinity School and the Yale School of the Environment. Frederica currently serves as the director of the Psychedelic Practitioner Training program at the Synthesis Institute, designing educational journeys for professionals in the fields of health, wellness, and personal transformation.

Claudia Jiménez is the minister of faith development with the Unitarian Universalist Congregation in Asheville, NC. She was director of religious education in Vero Beach, FL, for 17 years before moving to North Carolina. During that time, she also taught science, became a certified sexuality educator, served on numerous community boards, and ran for office, serving eight years on the school board. Claudia and her husband Steve are proud parents of two young adult daughters.

For type Three:

Celeste Collins is a one-breasted cancer survivor in her sixth decade of life. Although she resists labels (she feels they are dehumanizing and limiting), for the purpose of this book she identifies as white, cisgender female, progressive Christian. The beauty and wonder of creation give her energy and connection to the Holy. Celeste's career has been in banking and nonprofit leadership. After 30 years as executive director of OnTrack Financial Education and Counseling, she retired in 2023. She lives in Asheville, NC, with her husband Carleton, with whom she has two remarkable adult kids, Kathleen and Garrett.

Cyndi Gueswel founded Only to Grow (*www.onlytogrow.com*), a coaching and consulting business serving visionaries and leaders of social change. She specializes in 1:1 leadership coaching, cohort-based coaching, and transformative collaborations within teams. Cyndi is a Certified Narrative Enneagram Teacher and is accredited through Integrative Enneagram. Her passions are nature, art, poetry, music, community, and libraries.

For type Two:

Iyabo Onipede is a consultant and speaker who leads challenging yet compassionate learning experiences that promote thriving racial and cultural inclusion, equity, and belonging in organizations and communities. She also serves as the co-director of a nonprofit grassroots organization, Compassionate Atlanta, where she delights in loving on her diverse and eclectic community and where she is the most comfortable in her own skin. Iyabo's home on the web is *www.iamiyabo.com,* and you can connect with her at *hello@iamiyabo.com.*

Rev. Dr. Chelsea Brooke Yarborough was born and raised in Baltimore, MD. She is currently an assistant professor of liturgical studies at Garrett Evangelical Theological Seminary. Chelsea is an ordained minister, a poet, and an Enneagram coach. Her motto is "Live to love and love to live each day," and she is excited to continue her journey of cultivating and engaging curiosity in all that she pursues.

For type Four:

Dorrie Toney is a Queer woman with an MDiv from Emory University's Candler School of Theology. Her passion is helping people to embrace more authentic and connected lives by using the Enneagram, spiritual practices, and storytelling.

Cathy Wright, JD, is a retired attorney and consultant. After 25 years as a litigation attorney, she founded a consulting business working with clients ranging from international businesses to government and nonprofit organizations in planning change management, communication, and team development. Cathy is a Certified Narrative Enneagram Teacher. She is also certified by Tara Brach and Jack Kornfield as a Mindfulness Meditation Teacher. Cathy designs and teaches Mindfulness for people with physical disabilities in NCHPAD's MENTOR program. She is currently a Diamond Approach student in a group led by Sandra Maitri.

For type Six:

Beth Waltemath is a writer, writing coach, and ordained minister in Atlanta, GA. She loves helping people find their authentic voices as writers and authentic expressions of their spirituality. Her essays have appeared in the *New York Times*, the *Washington Post*, *CNN.com*, and *Chapter 16*. You can view her work, learn more about her coaching, and contact her through *bethwaltemath.com*.

Rev. Cathy Dempsey-Sims has been an Episcopal priest since 2008. She currently serves on the Bishop's staff for the partnership dioceses of Northwestern Pennsylvania and Western New York. Prior to entering the priesthood, Cathy served as a psychotherapist for more than 20 years.

For type Five:

As **Marilyn Coltrane** reflects on her life, she is filled with gratitude for the experience of being with children with severe disabilities and their families as a therapist for many years. They opened her mind and heart to the gifts of diversity in many forms. Since her retirement, she has shared these learnings in various small group settings, always hoping to create circles of care in her community.

Nicole McCreary lives in Columbia, SC. She is a devoted wife and mother and is currently employed with a local branch of an international nonprofit service organization. She serves as co-chair of the Board of Directors of the Columbia Children's Theatre.

For type Seven:

Zoë McCully is a transdisciplinary artist and substitute teacher lately working with clay, candles, and kids. They make whimsical, playful art that honors the fullness of the human experience. Zoë believes pleasure is our birthright and creates rituals in daily life and relationships that embody the deep desire to live in a more equitable world. They enjoy the outdoors, astrology, biking, and dancing.

Ann Rabin began her career dedicated to children and their families in nontraditional learning settings after she received an MS in psychology and special education. Ann committed herself to providing safe havens for youth, first in the classroom for challenged learners. As an education leader, she led a team that created innovative conservation education programs for children and families, opening the zoo world to first-time urban visitors and providing a niche for struggling adolescents. Fostering a collaborative approach, she joined community efforts to implement fair juvenile justice practices. Ann is a wife, mother, and grandmother and recently became an elder in a family of strong and independent women. Her role as primary caregiver for her husband, Larry, has been an ongoing quest to learn and love.

Acknowledgments

Attention is the rarest and purest form of generosity.
—SIMONE WEIL

When I read this quote from the mystic Simone Weil, the people who supported this endeavor immediately come to mind. I am grateful for the gift of their attention. Their detailed edits and thoughtful revisions inspired me (along with their honesty). In thinking of these dear people, the image of us "arm in arm" bringing this book to reality is vivid for me. You have been the keepers of possibility for me.

To the team at Hampton Roads Publishing whose "yes" transformed a manuscript into this book, I am so grateful. Your guidance, knowledge, and patience were wrapped in kindness. Michael Pye, after our first meeting, I knew I was in good hands. You got the heart of this book immediately. In a short time, I felt a kinship. My editor Rachel Head was simply extraordinary with spot-on edits offered in kindness.

Matt Bomhoff, you audaciously told me to write a book and that you would support me with editing. Thank you for believing in me so strongly that I believed this endeavor to be possible. Your thoughtful edits and encouragement were steadying throughout this process.

Much gratefulness to each of the Companion Voices who wrote, edited, and wrote more. Thank you for your patience and for sharing yourselves so beautifully. Your stories bring this book alive!

To those of you who read every word of this manuscript and offered affirmation, questions, critique, and edits, my heart is full of gratefulness. Thanks to Cyndi Gueswel, Marcia Tibbetts, Toby Brown, Linda Douty, and Annie Wills for attending to every word so graciously and in loving friendship. When doubt troubled me, you encouraged. Each of your suggestions moved me forward. You provided a kind container for me to stay the course. You are woven throughout this book.

To Ronda Redden Reitz, Eleanor McKenzie Delbene, and Karen Sanders, thank you for offering your time to brainstorm with me as we considered major themes and titles. For listening presence, prayers, humor, encouragement, and celebration, I leaned into Debbi Horton, Carol Dodson, Erlina Edwards, Mary Ann Watjen, Kathy Meunier, Gerry Fathauer, Anita Fletcher, Mary Beth Gwynn, Carol Taylor, Eli Corbin, and Linda Hemstreet. For just the right poem at just the right time, I'm grateful to you, Karen Abrams Gerber. For a timely morning conversation that meant more than you could know, thank you Carter Heyward. Rita Isbey, your loving friendship and prayers and your belief that this book would come alive have meant the world to me. My monthly Diamond Approach teacher Doriena Wolff constantly reminds me that I am much more than my type, and I appreciate your encouragement.

In the home stretch of this endeavor, Beth Waltemath taught me about thoroughness and how to better craft my thoughts. Thank you for challenging me to go deeper, to say more, to claim my knowing. You were a terrific writing coach and companion as I entered the publishing world. Thank you for your truth telling and your steadfastness.

Chris Pepple, you were an unexpected guide with just the right edits and recommendations. Thank you for your generosity in edits and suggestions. And Virginia Dupre, thank you for connecting me with Chris P. and for believing in this project and my Enneagram work throughout the years!

How does anyone write a book without logistical, legal, and technical support? Thank you to Tamara Sparacino for coming to my rescue early on to convert my work into an appropriate document. And Elaine Mayo, thank you for the detail with which you worked through the final manuscript. You were so gracious in your guidance through questions and encouragement. My friends Joann Klappauf and Steve Brown's knowledge of publishing supported me in thinking realistically about possibilities, and Steve, thank you for your work with the diagrams! Jerry Meunier, you offered me "legal love" and I'm grateful! And Suzanne Dion, thank you for your support from the beginning and for designing the beautiful graphic on this book's cover.

Leading me into new understandings of media and publicity wasn't easy, yet Vicki Murrell, Dorrie Toney, and Salem Bombace stayed the course with me through my stubbornness and my fears. Great gratitude!

Finally, my great appreciation goes to all of you who participated in my spirituality conversations and Enneagram type groups, panels, workshops, and more. You have been my teachers and made the Enneagram types real for me. In sharing yourselves, you grew my compassion. Thank you.

When anxiety blanketed me, the land of Western North Carolina soothed me. The trees returned me to my presence, the rivers reminded me to allow the unfolding.

Endnotes

Introduction

1 Audre Lorde, *Sister Outsider: Essays and Speeches* (Trumansburg, NY: Crossing Press, 1984), 10. The quote is from an interview in *The Feminist Renaissance*.

2 Brené Brown, *Rising Strong: The Reckoning. The Rumble. The Revolution.* (New York: Random House, 2015), 46.

Chapter 1

1 Terry Tempest Williams, *Erosion: Essays of Undoing* (New York: Sarah Crichton Books, 2019), xi.

Chapter 2

1 Jeanne de Salzmann, *The Reality of Being: The Fourth Way of Gurdjieff* (Boston, MA: Shambhala, 2011), 205.

Chapter 3

1 Samuel Lewis, *Spiritual Dance and Walk* (Seattle, WA: Peaceworks Intl. Network for the Dances of Universal Peace, 1996).

Chapter 4

1 Greg Jarrell, *A Riff of Love: Notes on Community and Belonging* (Eugene, OR: Cascade Books, 2018), xiii.

Chapter 5

1 David Gelles, "She's Taking on Elon Musk on Solar. And Winning," *New York Times*, January 23, 2020, *nytimes.com*.
2 Rumi, quoted in Michael Gurian, *The Soul of the Child: Nurturing the Divine Identity of Our Children* (New York: Atria Books, 2002), 14.

Chapter 10

1 Eckhart Tolle, *A New Earth: Awakening to Your Life's Purpose* (New York: Penguin, 2005), 274.

Chapter 11

1 Eckhart Tolle, *A New Earth: Awakening to Your Life's Purpose* (New York: Penguin, 2005), 190.

Chapter 12

1 Tim Ferriss, "Henry Shukman—Zen, Tools for Awakening, Ayahuasca vs. Meditation, Intro to Koans, and Using Wounds as the Doorway," *The Tim Ferriss Show* (podcast), September 8, 2021, *podcasts.apple.com*.

Chapter 13

1 Lao Tzu and Steven Mitchell, *Tao Te Ching* (New York: Harper & Row, 1988), 36.
2 The PAUSE Process emerged from my conversations with Ruth Hill, an Asheville Biodynamic Cranial Sacral Therapist.
3 Rumi, quoted in Akṣapāda, *The Analects of Rumi* (self-pub., 2019), 13.

Suggested Resources

The following resources provide additional information on Enneagram learning and deepening inner awareness. The marker ** indicates an introductory text.

Books:

Agoram, Chichi. *The Enneagram for Black Liberation*. Minneapolis, MN: Broadleaf, 2022.

Almaas, A.H. *Facets of Unity: The Enneagram of Holy Ideas*. Berkeley, CA: Diamond Books. 1998.

Almaas, A.H. *Keys to the Enneagram: How to Unlock the Highest Potential of Every Personality Type*. Boulder, CO: Shambala, 2021.

Blake, Amanda. *Your Body Is Your Brain*. Truckee, CA: Trokay Press. 2018.

** Chestnut, Bea. *The Complete Enneagram.* Ann Arbor, MI: She Writes Press, 2013.

Chestnut, Bea, and Uranio Paes. *The Enneagram Guide to Waking Up: Find Your Path, Face Your Shadow, Discover Your True Self.* Newburyport, MA: Hampton Roads, 2021.

Daniels, David, and Suzanne Dion. *The Enneagram, Relationships and Intimacy*. Self-published, 2018.

** Daniels, David, and Virginia Price. *The Essential Enneagram: The Definitive Personality Test and Self-Discovery Guide.* San Francisco, CA: HarperOne. 2000.

Egerton, Deborah Threadgill. *Know Justice Know Peace*. Carlsbad, CA: Hay House, 2022.

Gore, Belinda. *Finding Freedom: Understanding Our Relationships Using Object Relations and the Enneagram*. Columbus, OH: 2FriendsPress, 2023.

Lapid-Bogda, Ginger. *What Type of Leader Are You?* New York: McGraw-Hill, 2007.

Lapid-Bogda, Ginger. *The Enneagram Development Guide*. Self-published, 2012.

Maitri, Sandra. *The Spiritual Dimension of the Enneagram: Nine Faces of the Soul*. New York: Tarcher/Putnam, 2000.

Maitri, Sandra. *The Enneagram of Passions and Virtues*. New York: Tarcher/Penguin, 2005.

** Palmer, Helen. *The Enneagram: Understanding Yourself and the Others in Your Life*. San Francisco, CA: HarperCollins, 1988.

Palmer, Helen. *The Enneagram in Love and Work: Understanding Your Intimate and Business Relationships*. San Francisco, CA: HarperCollins, 1995.

Rhoades, Susan. *The Integral Enneagram*. Seattle, WA: Geranium Press, 2013.

** Riso, Don, and Hudson, Russ. *The Wisdom of the Enneagram*. New York: Bantam, 1999.

Zuercher, Suzanne. *Enneagram Companions: Growing in Relationships and Spiritual Direction*. Self-published, 2000.

Podcast:

Smith, Sandra, and Copeland, Chris. *Heart of the Enneagram*. *https://www.iheart.com/podcast/256-heart-of-the-enneagram-31120985/*.

About the Author

With over 20 years of teaching experience, author Sandra C. Smith weaves together her background in business and nonprofits with her theological education to offer a practical and compassionate exploration of the Enneagram's nine types. An accredited International Enneagram Association Professional and certified in the Narrative Enneagram Tradition, Sandra teaches internationally, inviting curiosity and compassion to guide the inward turn in exploring the foundational question, "Who am I?"

Whether in faith communities or corporate, nonprofit, or conference settings, Sandra identifies her key learning as *we humans are more alike than different*. Believing that understanding self and others is a key foundation for healthy development, her work engages people at their core, using silence, guiding questions, and stories as teachers. Interweaving the knowing of our three centers of intelligence—body, heart, and head—Sandra invites people into the possibility that *we are more than we believe ourselves to be*. She believes that our inner work is the starting point for our justice work. We are relational beings, and how we engage in relationships matters. For Sandra, the Enneagram is a powerful map guiding us toward healthy relationships and toward becoming compassionate participants in our world.

She has been shaped by her education at Wake Forest University, where she earned a BS in Business, and at Emory University's Candler School of Theology, where she received an MDiv. She has a certification in nonprofit management from Duke University and is a trained community mediator. A summer in India invited her to live more simply.

Sandra co-hosts the podcast *Heart of the Enneagram,* created to deepen our understanding of the Enneagram by listening to guests share their lived experiences of their Enneagram types.

Her life experience as female, identity as lesbian, love for the Earth, and commitment to equity and inclusion inform her teaching and her living.

Learn more about her work by visiting her website, *Alchemy WorksEvents.com.* Follow her on Instagram at *sandrasmith alchemyworks* and on Facebook at *facebook.com/alchemyworksevents.*

To Our Readers

HAMPTON ROADS PUBLISHING, an imprint of Red Wheel/Weiser, publishes inspirational books from a variety of spiritual traditions and philosophical perspectives for "the evolving human spirit."

Our readers are our most important resource, and we appreciate your input, suggestions, and ideas about what you would like to see published.

Visit our website at *www.redwheelweiser.com*, where you can learn about our upcoming books and also find links to sign up for our newsletter and exclusive offers.

You can also contact us at *info@rwwbooks.com* or at

Red Wheel/Weiser, LLC
65 Parker Street, Suite 7
Newburyport, MA 01950